Advance Praise for

Just Not That Likable

"Women who break the glass ceiling can find themselves bloodied in the process. Being effective as a woman often means confronting stereotypes and 'likeability' demands not made of men. As a trailblazer in policy and education, Dr. Romero has broken barriers and lived the consequences. Her book raises important questions for those of us working to ensure our daughters face more equitable paths to success and impact, paths that embrace their strength and temper the double standard we face."
—**Caprice Young, Ed.D,** National Superintendent, Lifelong Learning; Former Board of Education President, Los Angeles Unified School District; and Founding CEO, California Charter Schools Association

"Senator Romero exposes the persistence of gender inequity and workplace double standards still experienced by women. The book should be read as a call to action to state legislatures across the country to pass legislation mandating gender bias training, and stiffen penalties for those perpetuating impenetrable glass ceilings made of cement. As women are increasingly running for political offices and seeking entrance to leadership positions in both the private and public sectors, it is vital that we support these emerging women leaders. As the past Chair of the California Legislative Women's Caucus, I believe that we need to educate all girls with the understanding that these double-binds experienced by their grandmothers, mothers, and aunts will no longer be tolerated." —Hon. California State Senator **Connie M. Leyva**

"Senator Gloria Romero served as Senate Democratic Majority Leader of the California State Senate, the first woman to serve in that office in the upper house. Dr. Romero's dynamic legislative leadership was precursor to women subsequently becoming President of the Senate and Speaker of the Assembly. She influenced all major policy decisions affecting education, social justice, and access to government. This book pays homage—and is a tribute—to all the strong women for whom she advocated to no longer suffer the indignities and discriminatory behaviors still disturbingly present in today's workplaces." —Former President Pro Tempore of the California State Senate, **Don Perata**

"As an employment lawyer, I am shocked by the number of times a competent woman is told that she is too brash, too heavy-handed, or too demanding. Often, a man who exhibits the same characteristics is the one leveling these criticisms. And the employers rarely see it. Or if they do, they don't call it out. This book is another step towards bringing the necessary attention to these sexist double standards." —**David G. Greco,** Attorney, RMO LLP

"Throughout my professional career, because I am a woman, I was challenged to be better, to be stronger, to be more focused than my male counterpart. To do that, I had to project decisiveness, empathy, intellect and persistence. If I was perceived as selfish, opinionated and domineering-I figured it was their problem of perception and I defined their own sexism, classism and racism of the preceptor. Interesting dialog would ensue! Gloria Romero's interpretation in this book vindicates my perception of myself. I am a warrior and I am OK with it." —**Emma Lechuga,** Woman, Chicana, Educator, Entrepreneur

"An insightful, and well written book, that describes the obstacles and difficulties that women in leadership positions face when they strive to shatter gender and racial barriers. Gloria Romero has proven herself to be one of the most effective and passionate advocates for creating a stronger system for reporting and responding to sexual harassment and misconduct. This is a compelling and important book that provides a blueprint for a more inclusive future and serves as an inspiration for a new generation of public servants." —Hon. **Joe Coto,** Former California State Assemblymember and Chair Emeritus, of the California Latino Legislative Caucus; Superintendent of Schools in Oakland and San Jose

Just Not That Likable

The PRICE
ALL WOMEN PAY
for GENDER BIAS

Gloria J. Romero

FORMER CALIFORNIA SENATE MAJORITY LEADER

A POST HILL PRESS BOOK
ISBN: 978-1-64293-980-4
ISBN (eBook): 978-1-64293-981-1

Just Not That Likable:
The Price All Women Pay for Gender Bias
© 2021 by Gloria J. Romero
All Rights Reserved

Cover art by Cody Corcoran

Post Hill Press
New York • Nashville
posthillpress.com

Published in the United States of America
1 2 3 4 5 6 7 8 9 10

Special thanks to a new generation of young women willing, wanting, and able to call out gender bias and double standards when they see them. Thank you, Rachel Frankel and Jeslynn Mendoza, for helping me find the numerous research studies cited in this book. Thank you, Ramani Durvasula, for truly opening new doors for me to join other women in telling our stories. A special shout out to Post Hill Press. You've put me in the expert hands of Debra Englander and Heather King, who I absolutely enjoyed working with. I will never forget that email you sent me saying, "You are an author." Wow—and what a story I had to tell! Thank you for taking a chance on me. Thank you, also, to the wonderful editors Allie Woodlee and Jill Ezren for your encouragement and thoughtful insights.

A big hug to dear friends, colleagues, and sisters: Punam Grewal, Maribel Medina, Juana Mora, Jill Stewart, Kaveri Subrahmanyam, Cher Mendoza, and Caprice Young, who not only were there for me from the start, but who also, I know, will be there for anyone who has the courage to run—not walk—like a bull in a china shop through that labyrinth, swinging away at whatever glass ceilings portend to stand in our way.

As we know, there are no magic ruby slippers or golden brick roads to help us navigate through treacherous labyrinths and smash through seemingly impenetrable glass ceilings to get us safely home. But those ceilings and walls will come crashing down as we tell our stories, file our briefs, and sue our way to justice. There are always others who come before us, and I express my deepest gratitude to them for starting to pave those roads, making it less lonely or less of a road-less-traveled because of their courage to start the walk. May Ann

Hopkins, whom I never knew, rest in peace. Her life mattered for us all. Thank you, Ann Hopkins, for being so *unlikable* and changing history for every woman in this country who has the courage to not be afraid to speak up.

Finally, this book is for any woman who has ever been called bossy, mean, aggressive, or, quite frankly, just a bitch. As I once told my daughter, Soledad Ursua, all "bitch" means is that you stood up for yourself. More than anyone, this book is for her because she was the first one to encourage me to write it. Because of her, I refuse to wear pink on Wednesdays.

Table of Contents

Preface

Moderator: What can you say to the voters of New Hampshire on this stage tonight, who see your resume and like it, but are hesitating on the likability issue where they seem to like Barack Obama more?

Hillary Clinton: Well, that hurts my feelings.

Moderator: I'm sorry, Senator, I'm sorry.

Clinton: But I'll try to go on. He's very likable. I agree with that. I don't think I'm that bad.

Barack Obama: You're likable enough, Hillary.

-Hillary Clinton-Barack Obama presidential primary debate, January 5, 2008.

"If I didn't speak the way I do, I wouldn't have been seen as a leader. But my way of speaking may have grated on people who were not used to hearing it from a woman. It was the right way for a leader to speak, but it wasn't the right way for a woman to speak."

-Kim Campbell, first (and only) female prime minister of Canada, 1993.

"Even if we knew that (Ann) Hopkins had 'personality problems,' this would not tell us that the partners who cast their evaluations of Hopkins in sex-based terms would have criticized her as sharply (or criticized her at all) if she had been a man."

"We sit not to determine whether Ms. Hopkins is nice, but to decide whether the partners reacted negatively to her personality because she is a woman."

[In a landmark ruling for that Ann Hopkins being wrongly passed over for becoming a senior partner, the court wrote, "In the specific context of sex stereotyping, an employer who acts on the basis of a belief that a woman cannot be aggressive, or that she must not be, has acted on the basis of gender."]

-U.S. Supreme Court, in *Price Waterhouse v. Hopkins*, 1989.

"A dominant style won't convey competence or likability, and it often will make you seem ill tempered and out of control. Although women seldom use a domineering style, be on the alert for any tendencies you might have in this direction—and check them."

-Andrea S. Kramer and Alton B. Harris, *Breaking Through Bias: Communication Techniques for Women to Succeed at Work* (Boston: Nicholas Brealey Publishing, second edition, p. 108, 2020.

"So arm yourself with the knowledge of these pages, ladies. Be vigilant about hiding yourself. (Not your entire self, just the woman and/or minority part of yourself.) Scale the heights of your career and break that glass ceiling, but do it very quietly and gingerly, and be sure to make a man think he did it for you. By standing as still as possible, you will go farther than you ever imagined, as long as you didn't imagine going too far."

-Sarah Cooper, *How to Be Successful Without Hurting Men's Feelings: Non-Threatening Leadership Strategies for Women* (Andrews McMeel Publishing, p. 5, 2018).

Once upon a time, I was told: "Gloria, you come out of the Legislature where women are expected to be strong, but this is a workplace where women are weak. This is a mismatch."

-Gloria Romero

CONTRIBUTOR

It was 1970, a year before eighteen-year-olds got the vote in America, when forty-six female staffers at *Newsweek* filed the first gender discrimination lawsuit against a U.S. employer, a case won by a brilliant young attorney, Eleanor Holmes Norton. Called "dollies" by their male bosses and informed that women "don't write," the *Newsweek* women were stuck with menial jobs for which they were overqualified. They cut a new path taken twelve years later by Ann Hopkins, a senior manager at then-Price Waterhouse, who in 1982 sued her firm for passing her over for a partnership despite her stellar work. Hopkins's disgust and grit resulted in a monumental U.S. Supreme Court ruling in 1989 that changed everything: the highest court in the nation, which included the first woman justice, decisively clarified that employers could no longer evaluate employees based on stereotypes.

Hopkins's name, once common in news outlets' front pages, is today unknown to most Americans. But author, educator, and former legislator Gloria Romero, the first woman to hold the powerful seat of Democratic Majority Leader of the California State Senate, brings Hopkins back in *Just Not That Likable* as the penultimate female warrior in a sprawling—and clearly unfinished—war against women in America's executive offices.

Four decades after Price Waterhouse v. Hopkins, *Just Not That Likable* lays out the devastating argument that a pervasive fog of bias persists today, a softer but equally ugly and destructive denigration of women who gain or seek power in America's corporations and organizations. In unpacking this thriving yet more subtle form of gender bias than the open discrimination Ann Hopkins confronted, Romero delves into the outrageous "likability" standards widely applied—but rarely acknowledged—to women in the twenty-first century.

Romero points to the emergence of modern-era trailblazers such as Uber whistleblower Susan Fowler and former Reddit CEO Ellen Pao, who unsuccessfully took on her venture capital employer, Kleiner Perkins, for gender discrimination. Although Pao lost in court, "She won over the hearts and minds of women everywhere who understand that hers was a good fight and her fight has made it possible for others to have courage as well," the author writes.

But women are often judged and held back today if they fail to conform to unspoken likability standards. Romero warns that such rising practices as "pay-for-performance," which lack objective measurements that keep pace, "will rely on heuristics and likability traits to determine performance and pay—factors which, as we've seen, have double standards for women."

Laying out a series of steps to fight and undo America's unspoken "likability" standards, *Just Not That Likable* is an insightful, angry, vivid, and ultimately practical guidebook to beating today's gender discrimination, which quietly thrives in institutions, firms, and the psyches of the executives who run them.

Jill Stewart, Los Angeles, former managing editor at *LA Weekly*
Twitter: @jillstewart

CONTRIBUTOR

It is unfortunate that in 2021, there remains a dire need to write a book addressing the lack of awareness of discriminatory stereotypes against women whom most would describe as "strong." But the need is there. Dr. Gloria Romero—the college professor, former Majority Leader in the California State Senate, and just all-around amazing woman—is just the person to write this book, giving a voice to any woman who has ever been penalized for being strong.

"Hola mujer" is Gloria's signature greeting. "Mujer," meaning woman, may as well be translated for the word "warrior." I would be hard-pressed to think of a conversation I have had with Gloria in the past two decades where we were not discussing being the "first." During the time she served as a senator, I sought her support to obtain the position of the top legal counsel for one of the largest public entities in the United States. Her immediate response was, "Of course, would you be the first Latina in that position?" And, of course, the answer was yes.

Over her career, Gloria has demonstrated an acute ability to analyze, synthesize, and enact changes, particularly to provide the American dream and educational opportunities for children of color. Gloria always encouraged the people who worked for her to dream big. Her former chief of staff is now a superior court judge.

Shockingly, her amazing work ethic, intelligence, and fortitude turned into a liability, resulting in conversations over her being termed "too aggressive" or "not nice," or having to face criticism that she actually expected people to reach the same high standards expected of all. Ironically, there was zero self-awareness from the individuals making those assertions that the statements were sexist.

And sadly, I could have had similar conversations with most of the "strong" women I know.

What is disturbing to me, as a lawyer, is that I have worked in both public and private sector law throughout California and have chaired education law practice groups. I have served as legal counsel in the two largest school systems in California. I graduated from one of the most prestigious law schools, Berkley School of Law, and received my master's degree in public administration from Harvard.

As *Just Not That Likable* explains, the more competent a woman is, the less her colleagues tend to like her. In addition to the emotional toll this type of reverse aggravation takes on the woman, it creates significant barriers to professional promotions or, in some instances, a complete bar to certain positions. This is seen, for example, in the vetting of potential judges who will actually hear case evidence of sex discrimination claims from women seeking justice. How this works in California is not unlike how it works nationally: surveys of the potential "suitability" of a potential judge are sent to thousands of lawyers, including those who are opposing counsel. If the case involves a multimillion-dollar matter or someone's job or reputation, it is very likely the case will be incredibly adversarial. In a perfect world, if you won, the opposing counsel would shake your hand and say, great job. But guess what? In the real world, the losing lawyer may not be very pleased. The surveys are a perfect opportunity to get even. As this book illustrates, if you happen to be a woman, worse yet, a *minority* woman, don't be surprised when the feedback is negative: she is aggressive, not very smart, lacks the proper temperament—in other words, just not that likable to sit on the bench.

These comments made of minority judicial candidates with Ivy League educations and brilliant minds who have served as counsel to some of the most complex public entities can leave one dumbfounded. As an attorney, I am accustomed to asking, "Where is the evidence?" when receiving claims that appear drastically different from known facts. As this book highlights, no evidence is necessary. If the resume begins with the name Heidi instead of Howard, the educational and professional accomplishments will be viewed differently. I recall one particular instance when an individual had my resume in front of him and said, "Well, it does not appear you're very smart." My response: "Would you reconsider that conclusion if you simply replaced the name Maribel Medina with Joe Smith?"

This book is a must-read for any woman—not just those who lead law firms or corporate suites or school districts. In order to make change, Gloria says we need to "get over the need to be liked." The advice, however, is challenging without true institutional change. It is no wonder that there are such few minority women serving as judges on the bench. It is no wonder that there are such few women—and even fewer minority women—serving as executives at every level. Yet, the laws are there, and it is incumbent for all women to learn them and feel empowered and supported to actually use them. If there is a true desire to diversify institutions such as the bench, corporate suites, and schools at every level, then this book is a must-read.

Maribel S. Medina, Partner
Leal & Trejo, APC
Twitter: @maribelmlaw

CHAPTER ONE

To the Glass Ceiling and Beyond (Ouch, That Hurts!)

Once upon a time in my career—and not unlike many other successful women in America—I was summoned to a meeting with my employer. In that meeting long, long ago, after questioning me for two hours, the corporate "suits" simply declared, "Gloria, you served in the California State Legislature where women are expected to be strong. But this is a workplace where women are weak. This is a mismatch."

mis·match

noun

/mis-maCH/

a failure to correspond or match; a discrepancy.
"a huge mismatch between supply and demand"
Similar: discrepancy, lack of congruence ,inconsistency, contradiction

verb

/mis-maCH/

match (people or things) unsuitably or incorrectly.
"designers throw in big furniture pieces that are deliberately mismatched with the existing ones to give an accent to the space"
Similar: ill-assorted, ill-matched, incongruous, unsuited, incompatible

Indeed, I had served as a member of the California State Legislature, rising to become the first woman in California history to be elected as the Senate Majority Leader. Along the way, I had written legislation defending women and had mentored young women to stand up for themselves. I had marched and rallied for human rights, and never shied away from standing up for what is fair and just. I sought results and expected them of myself and anyone I supervised.

As I sat in that conference room, I realized that they were pronouncing me *just not that likable*—my voice, my mannerisms, my directness, my high standards and no-nonsense sense of leadership. Was I a successful, respected, and strong leader? Yes. But was

I likable? According to them, no. Wow! I hadn't seen that coming, even though as a university professor emeritus, I sometimes lectured on *this very issue* impacting women leaders and the growing body of research exposing the double bind women face: expectations that we'll be strong, followed by punishment for not being likable.

lik·a·ble

/ˈlīkəb(ə)l/

adjective

adjective: **likable**

(especially of a person) pleasant, friendly, and easy to like.
"a very likable young woman"

Similar: pleasant, nice, friendly, agreeable, affable, amiable, genial

In my "once upon a time" story, I turned to the assembled corporate "suits" and asked, "Tell me, where in the job description does it say strong women need not apply nor lead this organization?" followed by a satirical, "Should I start wearing pink on Wednesdays? How demure would you like me to speak?"

I left the meeting and immediately called a dear friend, who counseled me to speak with a lawyer. Welcome to life in the executive suite, she said, where women are still expected to "act girlie" in order to succeed.

So here I am, a "strong" woman who—despite my professional record of accomplishments—has been chastised for, essentially, not behaving like a lady. Like the five stages of grief identified by Elisabeth Kübler-Ross, I experienced denial, anger, bargaining, depression, and finally acceptance over this realization. Knowing that I am not the first strong woman to be reprimanded for being strong, nor will I likely be the last, I started writing this book.

Is it possible for a woman to be strong *and* likable? When women lead, must we retreat to the pink ghetto and seek seclusion in a gender closet to avoid our authentic selves? Despite decades of advancements and the passage of key nondiscriminatory legislation, are we condemned to continue paying a "likability" penalty or lose our jobs and have to sue our employers? What do we tell our daughters when we talk about taking down discriminatory glass ceilings when the very behaviors required for them to lead are perceived as "difficult," "abrasive," "bossy," and "selfish"?

In a word, *unlikable.*

Like the B-word many of us have heard (you know, the one that rhymes with witch), *unlikable* is a label women have long faced in the workplace, whether directed toward ourselves, a female colleague, a female politician, a female CEO, or most female political figures—women with power. Certainly, the progress of a robust American women's rights movement and modern-day feminism, aided by gender-equalizing legislation, has helped mitigate *overt* workplace sexism. But despite these advancements, the perpetuation of gender stereotypes remains pervasive, impacting women everywhere.

Fifty years ago, the *Harvard Business Review* found that 41 percent of survey respondents reported being "anti-woman executive" in principle, and only about a quarter reported feeling comfortable working for a woman.[1]

Today, we are not as likely to uncover such stark opinions from survey respondents about being blatantly anti-woman executive. But guess what? I hate to be the bearer of bad news, but when we get to Chapter Two, we will see that most of us—male and female—*still* say we prefer a male boss. Fifty years hasn't changed that.

---

1   Deborah L. Rhode, *Women and Leadership* (New York: Oxford University Press, 2017), 56.

Indeed, three decades ago we were warned, "Many women have paid their dues, even a premium, for a chance at a top position, only to find a glass ceiling between them and their goal. The glass ceiling is not simply a barrier for an individual, based on the person's inability to handle a higher-level job. Rather, the glass ceiling applies to women as a group who are kept from advancing higher *because they are women.*"[2]

According to Catalyst, a leading nonprofit research organization working to advance women in business, despite gains in the number of Fortune 500 women CEOs in 2020, there are only thirty-seven—out of 500![3] At the time of this writing, there are still nearly thirteen companies run by a man for every company run by a woman. Within the ranks of the thirty-seven women, a long-standing problem persists: there is starkly little racial diversity. Only three of the thirty-seven are women of color. Not one of the 500 companies on this list has a Black woman at the helm. While the overall picture—that women run 7.4 percent of the businesses on the Fortune 500—is significant, there are some more micro trends worth noting. Many of these women leaders are concentrated at the bottom of the Fortune 500, where the companies are smaller. Only seven women run Fortune 100 companies.

Furthermore, women are falling behind early in their careers. If first-level women managers were hired and promoted like men, there would be one million more women in management over the next five years. And to even get to this point means women have

---

2   Ann Morrison, Randall P. White, Ellen Van Velsor, and The Center for Creative Leadership, *Breaking the Glass Ceiling: Can Women Reach the Top of America's Largest Corporations?* (Boston: Addison-Wesley Pub. Co., 1989), 13.

3   The Fortune 500 is an annual list compiled and published by *Fortune* magazine that ranks 500 of the largest United States corporations by total revenue for their respective fiscal years. The list includes publicly held companies, along with privately held companies for which revenues are publicly available.

had to face barriers in landing their first management roles—much less remaining and prospering there.[4] The proverbial glass ceiling remains intact, sturdy, and strong.

In the United States, women were nearly half (47 percent) of the labor force but only slightly over a third (40 percent) of managers in 2019. That same year, White women held almost a third (32.3 percent) of all management positions. In the coveted C-suite of executive leadership, 21 percent of its members are women, but only 4 percent are women of color. Specifically, women of color held a drastically smaller share of management positions—Latinas, 4.3 percent; Black women, 4 percent; Asian women, 2.5 percent. Not even Catalyst reports on Native American women.

Ponder that women represent a third of MBA graduates, but only 4 percent of Fortune 500 CEOs. There are more men named John running S&P 1500 companies than there are women of any name. In finance and insurance, women make up almost half of middle managers but only 17 percent of senior managers in the largest firms. Globally, women hold less than a quarter of senior management roles, the stepping-stone to CEO positions. And in the United States, women of color account for 19 percent of the population but only 4 percent of the executives or senior-level management in S&P companies. A Catalyst report summarized the situation in its title: "Still No Progress After Years of No Progress."[5]

The conclusion? It could take more than a century to achieve parity in executive suites.[6] Other estimates are significantly more pessimistic, projecting it will take 400 years for women to reach just

4   "Quick Take: Women in Management," Catalyst, posted August 11, 2020,
     https://www.catalyst.org/research/women-in-management/.
5   "Catalyst 2013 Census of Fortune 55: Still No Progress After
     Years of No Progress," New York, Catalyst, 2013.
6   Deborah L. Rhode, *Women and Leadership* (New York: Oxford University Press, 2017), 57.

50 percent of the CEO positions,[7] while the Women in the Workplace 2018 study estimates parity in 450 years![8]

Closing these gaps is critical for women. While there are several factors to explain the underrepresentation, there is no getting around the perceived "mismatch" between the qualities *associated with leadership* and the qualities *viewed as attractive* in women. Most characteristics associated with leadership are masculine-oriented: dominance, authority, assertiveness, and so forth.

"The dragon lady" comes to mind. Or bitch. Or bossy. Quite frankly, all imply that she's *just not that likable* and all women pay the price for this continued gender bias.

Traditional gender stereotypes still leave women with a double standard and a double bind. *She's* abrasive, but *he's* assertive. Aggressive women are viewed as unpleasant to work with or for and have difficulty enlisting respect, support, and cooperation from coworkers.

Assertive is defined as having or showing a confident and forceful personality; however, when a female is assertive, it can be defined as abrasive, which has a negative connotation and refers to showing little concern for the feelings of others.

Let's face it: women are expected to work in narrower emotional channels than men. In order for a woman to be more attractive, she's not only encouraged to use Botox for her face, but also use a workplace Botox to constrain her authentic self while on the job! In environments where men are dominating and confrontational, women in that same environment risk being dismissed as pushy, bossy, abrasive, bitchy, and unlikable. In one tech field study, these criticisms showed up only twice in eighty-four critical reviews received by men, but in

7   Nancy E. Parsons, *Women Are Creating the Glass Ceiling and Have the Power to End It* (New York: WSA Publishing, 2019).
8   "Women in the Workplace 2018," McKinsey & Company and LeanIn. Org, 2018, https://womenintheworkplace.com/2018.

seventy-one of the ninety-four critical reviews received by women. Eighty-four percent of women received job performance feedback that they were too aggressive, with female employees receiving two-and-a-half times the amount of feedback as their male colleagues concerning an aggressive communication style.[9]

Carly Fiorina, who was fired from being CEO of Hewlett-Packard, stated, "After striving my entire career to be judged by results and accomplishments, the coverage of my gender, my appearance and the perceptions of my personality would vastly outweigh anything else."[10]

Geraldine Laybourne, once president of Disney/ABC Cable Networks, when asked whether then-Mattel CEO Jill Barad was too abrasive, unabashedly responded by asking, "[Have they]…met Ted Turner? Have they met Michael Eisner? Compared to most CEOs she is not abrasive. But maybe compared to their wives she is."[11]

Psychologists, sociologists, and political scientists are on to this, and a growing body of academic research articles have documented this discrepancy between stereotypically feminine traits and traits considered necessary for leadership. These treatises have found that women are typically stereotyped as being *communal* (e.g., caring, soft, interdependent) and less *agentic* (e.g., ambitious, direct, competitive, capable, self-reliant) than men. Thus, there is a *mismatch* between what women are *thought* to be like, and what leadership is *thought* to require.

Women in the workplace often find themselves having to balance themselves as unambiguously agentic to ensure they are perceived to be as competent as men in executive, leadership positions. However, simultaneously, women face interpersonal penalties when they

---

9   Deborah L. Rhode, *Women and Leadership* (New York: Oxford University Press, 2017), 61.
10   Deborah L. Rhode, *Women and Leadership* (New York: Oxford University Press, 2017), 57.
11   Deborah L. Rhode, *Women and Leadership* (New York: Oxford University Press, 2017), 61.

exhibit such agency. Agentic women may be rated as highly competent and capable of leadership but are viewed as socially deficient by both male and female evaluators. It's sort of like a Dr. Jekyll and Mr. Hyde phenomenon!

This leads to women being labeled unlikable and suffering hiring or promotion penalties. In contrast, identically self-promoting male applicants are viewed as highly competent, likable, and hirable—unlike when women exhibit similar self-promoting behaviors, which provoke backlash.[12]

And be it corporate America or educational institutions, the key issue is women who lead, women executives, women with power. *Women perceived as strong.* One report seeking to understand the paucity of female leaders in education settings found that the most frequent barrier identified by women was the different expectations for men and women in leadership roles, writing: "One such norm was the sense that women did not match"—*there's that word again!*—"the traditional standard of 'being presidential'...while men were assumed to be competent."[13] Overall, men do not face the same pressure as women to overcome stereotypic expectations to succeed in the workplace. Agentic characteristics needed for leadership work for men...not so much for women.

Right out of the gate, research has shown that female applicants must first combat sex discrimination to land the job and then be wary of the leadership skills they utilize as they advance. Women are often forced to choose between promotion disqualification for

---

12   Deborah L. Rhode, *Women and Leadership* (New York: Oxford University Press, 2017), 12.
13   Kelly Hannum, Shannon Muhly, Pamela Shockley-Zalabak, and Judith S. White, "Stories From the Summit Trail: Leadership Journeys of Senior Women in Higher Education," Higher Education Resource Services, August 2014, 16, https://hers-network.org/wp-content/uploads/2018/08/StoriesfromtheSummitTrail.pdf.

being insufficiently competent or insufficiently feminine when they compete for leadership roles.

Over time, all women pay the price for this likability factor. When women manage to crack the glass ceiling and are hired for a management position, backlash results in gender discrimination at all stages of women's careers, including salary negotiations, performance evaluations, and promotion decisions. In this way, the cumulative effects of penalizing female agency are likely to have a substantial impact on women's ability to achieve the highest levels of leadership and professional success, dampening women's aspirations to even try. Thus, understanding the professional consequences of backlash is an essential step toward achieving gender parity in the workplace.

Women make up less than a quarter of America's prized "corner offices"—the esteemed executive C-suites—despite a college graduation rate superior to their male counterparts. Women earn 20 percent lower wages despite holding identical qualifications to their (higher-paid) male colleagues.

And consider these statistics:[14]

- 42 percent of women experience gender discrimination at work;

- in 2017, 25,000 sex-based discrimination claims were filed;

- in 2018, victims of sex-based discrimination received more than $148 million in payouts from complaints;

- both men and women are twice as likely to hire a male candidate;

- men are 30 percent more likely to obtain managerial roles;

- 23 percent of CEOs are women;

---

14   Bailey Reiners, "What Is Gender Bias in The Workplace?," BuiltIn, October 9, 2019, updated February 18, 2021, builtin.com/diversity-inclusion/gender-bias-in-the-workplace.

- 4 percent of C-suite roles are held by women of color;

- 6.6 percent of CEOs at Fortune 500 companies are women;

- 0.2 percent of CEOs at Fortune 500 companies are women of color.

Unlike the overt sexism of yesterday that prohibited women from entering leadership positions, the more subtle—dare I say a gentlemanly, benevolent sexism—of today upends women who have entered that formerly "for men only" club by punishing us for succeeding under the double standard of being insufficiently feminine and, therefore, *just not that likable*! The likability penalty imposes a severe professional and mental health tax on women. Having done everything right to succeed in what once was culturally and legally considered "a man's world," women are haunted by charges such as, "You're too strong," "Your voice is shrill," "You're too pushy," "You're not feminine enough." Quite frankly, you're just a bitch and we don't like you.

This is workplace whiplash!

These biases exist even as women exercise leadership roles in all sectors of the economy and across the political spectrum. In the electoral arena, women make up more than half of voters but only 19 percent of Congress and 12 percent of governors. A woman has never been elected president, though several have tried. As I write, a woman has just been elected as vice president of the United States. Yet, she was quickly labeled "a monster," "nasty," and "not likable." The U.S. ranks ninety-seventh in the world for representation of women in political office. In higher education, women are a majority of college graduates and postgraduate students, but only a quarter of full-time professors and university presidents. Women make up almost half of law school graduates, but only 18 percent of equity partners at major firms and 21 percent of Fortune 500 general counsels.

In business, women are opening small businesses on Main Street at a faster pace than ever before. But on Wall Street and as CEOs, they are still disproportionately limited.

Undeniably, women are striving to attain—and landing—leadership roles. The challenge, however, is *staying* there and leading without being subjected to expectations of what a woman leader looks or sounds like. Some self-help books urge women to tap their "feminine" side in order to survive—in other words, to change rather than tackle structural and cultural issues in the workplace. I was aghast to see one book on Amazon.com entitled *How to Be Successful Without Hurting Men's Feelings: Non-threatening Leadership Strategies for Women*. However, once I read it, I laughed out loud, since it's written as a humorous account of how women would, seemingly, need to transform themselves in order to succeed. Other academic-minded volumes on women and leadership give serious attention to what women must do to succeed and make themselves "attractive" in order to be included, successful, and liked in the old-boys club.

Navigating the leadership labyrinth has resulted in advising women on everything from voice tone to hand mannerisms to how intently we look at staff we supervise.

So even in a new era when women run for the presidency or vice presidency of the United States—and win—we are still being cautioned to "stand down." To just be *likable*…even if it means wearing different makeup, speaking softly, or diverting our eyes when speaking to a subordinate…or wearing pink on Wednesdays.

Some women and leadership volumes present sanitized "communication techniques" for women to succeed at work.[15] One published in 2016—the same year in which a woman, Hillary Clinton, ran for President of the United States of America—acknowledges the reality of gender bias but goes on to essentially *blame the victim* and encourage women to reshape themselves. For example, when giving advice to women appearing dominant, they warn women to "be on the alert" for any tendencies she might have toward a dominant style of leadership and to "check these."

Until recently, the U.S. Air Force distributed a Sexual Assault Prevention and Response guide, advising women that when attacked, it might be better to submit than fight back. That same paradox exists in corporations as well, though not quite as apparent. Females who fight back or stand up for themselves are often shunned or unwelcomed. But the days of telling us to just lie back and enjoy it—or at least tolerate it—are over. Umm, no. I don't think so, and thankfully, almost every "strong" woman to whom I spoke in a leadership capacity while writing this book revealed to me that she, too, had been accused of being "mean" at her workplace. Quite frankly, none of my male colleagues in executive roles tell me they were reprimanded for

---

15   Andrea S. Kramer and Alton B. Harris, *Breaking Through Bias: Communication Techniques for Women to Succeed at Work* (Brookline, MA: Bibliomotion, Inc., 2016).

being "strong," or standing while speaking, or looking directly into the eyes of a subordinate. They're not even described as "strong"— they just *are*, and no qualifications are needed. Men are licensed to exert and exude power and authority, and to be agentic in their personality and leadership styles.

Workplace negativity toward agentic women results in the punishment and banishment of similarly styled women. Double bind. Double standard. Researchers call it "the Goldilocks Dilemma— women having to try to figure out what is 'just right' to succeed in the job."[16] I was amazed at how many chapters and articles I read that cautioned us to think about how our strength can intimidate others— but these articles are directed at women, not men. I wonder if these "women and leadership" volumes might just urge us to becomse Stepford wives, the depiction of submissive women not only transformed but even physiologically rewired to become sweet, compliant, submissive women in the 1975 classic film by the same name.

The good news is that women are talking—in research labs, at women's conferences, online, in blogs, and in the proverbial ladies rooms where we're comparing what we've been told by our corporate suits. Increasingly, that L word—*likability*—is gaining cache in understanding why *He* can be free to be the leader we perceive and expect him to be, but *She* cannot.

Ultimately, that's the problem with the likability debate: it's being held in the unfair context of sexist perceptions we still maintain and uphold. In an illuminating column in *Forbes Women*, author Carrie Kerpen challenges us to ponder what's wrong with this personality ghetto into which women are still pigeonholed. After all, she asserts, it shouldn't be unlikable for a woman to be tough and assertive. It

---

16   Andrea S. Kramer and Alton B. Harris, *Breaking Through Bias: Communication Techniques for Women to Succeed at Work* (Brookline, MA: Bibliomotion, Inc., 2016), 76.

shouldn't be unlikable for a woman to be decisive and confident. It shouldn't be unlikable for a woman to be honest. It shouldn't be unlikable for a woman to be human.[17]

So, this book is written for all women who have been called the dreaded B word, or dragon lady, bossy, witchy, abrasive, shrill, manly, and, quite frankly, *just not that likable*! It's also written for all women who have never been called any of those terms—*so far*! Just wait. Your next advancement might launch you into the Not Likable Club, and this book might just come in handy as you traverse that labyrinth and smash your way out. The good news is that, increasingly, women are challenging these double binds and choosing authenticity over giving in and wearing pink on Wednesdays in an effort to just lie back and take it to survive in the C-suite. While some authors have suggested that women succumb to gender bias and just try to become more likable, others challenge the belief that women need to change themselves in order to "go along to get along." For example, in a fabulous and humorous treatise on the topic, Jessica Bennett argues for the creation of Feminist Fight Clubs[18] for women to understand tactical strategies to not just survive sexist workplaces, but to dismantle them for good. (Is that the *Rocky* theme song I hear playing?) I suggest further strategies and tactics that women can take to fight gender bias in Chapter Six.

---

17 Carrie Kerpen, "What's Wrong With Being a Likeable Woman?" *Forbes Women*, February 26, 2019.

18 Jessica Bennett, *Feminist Fight Club* (New York: HarperCollins, 2017).

Progress and advancement for women should not resemble Pan's Labyrinth with special instructions on how to survive without being condemned to Dante's hell. Despite the challenges, women have always stood up for our sex, asking no special favors. Women have long led our families, organizations, states and nations. Organizations that lack a culture of equal opportunity are less able to attract, retain, and motivate the most qualified individuals.[19] Even something as mundane as a job description contains traces of unconscious bias. Language inherently has gendered associations, so including words like "confident," "strong," "outspoken," and "decisive" have

---

19   "Report: 2001 Catalyst Census of Women Board Directors," Catalyst, posted December 4, 2001, https://www.catalyst.org/research/2001-catalyst-census-of-women-board-directors/.

been found to attract male candidates and deter female candidates, setting up obstacles to women's success from the jump. And once on the job, those same desired characteristics are more likely to be used against women who exhibit them! As you read this book, you will see that women have been confronting double standards at work by all means necessary, including filing gender bias claims and lawsuits. A critical mass of consciousness is brewing.

We cannot afford to exclude talented, intelligent leaders from positions of influence due to persistent gender biases still deeply embedded in our workplaces and society. Strong, gutsy, smart women make a difference at the workplace. Gender bias hurts all women and girls, not just the ones who are gaining access to executive suites. And women should not be told to change who we are in order to succeed. And having to wear pink on Wednesdays should not be handed down to us from any of the corporate suits calling us into conference rooms. Chimamanda Ngozi Adichie, author of *We Should All Be Feminists*, advises, "If you start thinking about being likable you are not going to tell your story honestly, because you are going to be so concerned with not offending, and that's going to ruin your story, so forget about likability."[20]

I'll toast to that! So, let's turn the page.

---

20   Allison P. Davis, "Here's Some Solid Advice: Forget About Being 'Likable,'" The Cut, posted May 29, 2015, https://www.thecut.com/2015/05/solid-advice-forget-about-being-likable.html.

CHAPTER TWO

On the Basis of Gender: We Like Him, Not Her

Leave it to Shakespeare to identify what might be the definitive question determinative of female executives' success in today's world when he swooningly muses, "What's in a name? That which we call a rose by any other name would smell as sweet."

That classic balcony scene might have inspired love when the Bard wrote *Romeo and Juliet* in the sixteenth century, but over the centuries we have learned that a name absolutely matters, especially if that name happens to be suggestive of our gender.

Leave it to university researchers to pick up where Shakespeare left off when, in 2003, they designed and conducted a groundbreaking study that showed the world that even when women smash the glass ceiling and find a seat at the leadership table, we still confront barriers restricting our advancement. Frank Flynn and Cameron Anderson of Columbia Business School and New York University, respectively, tested the "rose by any other name would smell as sweet" hypothesis, utilizing perceptions of the success and likability of men and women in the workplace.[21] For their study, the researchers utilized the résumé of a real-life female entrepreneur named Heidi Roizen, who had become a successful venture capitalist by using her "outgoing personality...and vast personal and professional network [that] included many of the most powerful business leaders in the technology sector."

The woman's real name, Heidi, was placed on one set of identical résumés, and a man's name, Howard (a perceived male), on another. In a cleverly designed study, Flynn and Anderson then assigned half of their research participants to read Heidi's profile and gave the other half "Howard's"—the exact same profile.

---

21   Kathleen L. McGinn and Nicole Tempest, *Heidi Roizen*, Harvard Business School Case Study #9-800-228 (Boston: Harvard Business School Publishing, 2009).

The result was remarkable: in respondents' evaluations of Heidi and Howard, participants rated both as equally competent—an unsurprising finding given that their accomplishments were completely identical. But then the findings dramatically diverged: Although Heidi and Howard were both respected, Howard was judged a more appealing colleague. Heidi was seen as aggressive, selfish, and not "the type of person you would want to hire or work for." She wasn't a "team player" nor was she someone with whom they'd like to work. Study respondents were much harsher on Heidi than on Howard across the board, making it clear that they *just did not like her.*

Conclusion: we like Howard; we don't like Heidi.

But why? With the exact same credentials, background, and accomplishments and with only the name changed, Howard was judged to be likable and a good colleague, someone people wanted to work with, while Heidi was not. The likability schism seems to have been driven on the basis of gender. The more assertive they thought Heidi was, the more harshly they judged her, disliking her aggressive personality. However, when the *exact* characteristics were ascribed to a perceived male, respondents championed and embraced him.

DRAWING QUIZ: HONESTLY...WHAT DO YOU THINK HOWARD LOOKS LIKE? HEIDI?

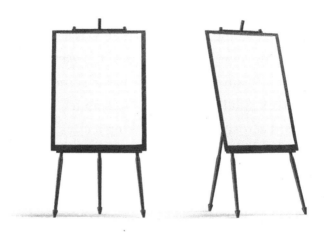

Howard is a rose. But, alas, Heidi has thorns. Avoid her at all costs. Do not hire her....

Undoubtedly, Sheryl Sandberg is a highly successful woman. As the chief operating officer of Facebook, she is ranked on *Fortune's* list of the 50 Most Powerful Women in Business and as one of *Time's* 100 Most Influential People in the World. She writes, "When a man is successful, he is liked by both men and women. When a woman is successful, people of both genders like her less. This truth is both shocking and unsurprising: shocking because no one would ever admit to stereotyping on the basis of gender and unsurprising because clearly we do,"[22] exposing biases and double standards affecting women in the corporate world. To her credit, Sandberg

---

22 Sheryl Sandberg, *Lean In: Women, Work, and the Will to Lead* (New York: Alfred A. Knopf, 2013), 40.

devotes a chapter of her bestseller, *Lean In: Women, Work, and the Will to Lead* to the issue of "Success and Likeability." But that's only one chapter! So much more work is needed to illuminate the reality of why likability impacts all women in the workplace.

The classic Heidi/Howard study demonstrates the inherent bias that people hold about typical gender roles and behaviors, and how men and women are judged by different rules, even when they are *equally competent*. And since then, research has continued to document the chasm in how employers, colleagues, and us ourselves view "strong" women. Unfortunately, this body of research on women and leadership produces findings underscoring the challenging beliefs we hold about women's advancement: success and likability are *positively* correlated for men but *negatively* correlated for women. In other words, our cultural stereotype of men holds that they are decisive, driven, in charge. For men, professional success seems to come with positive reinforcement every step of the way. We *expect* men to succeed. We *expect* men to lead. We *expect* men to be in charge, to command, even to demand. But for women? Not so much. Indeed, one of the most pernicious and persistent barriers to women's advancement is the "mismatch"—(*there's that word I've heard!*)—between qualities associated with *leadership*, as opposed to qualities associated with *women*.[23]

Our cultural stereotypes of women are different. We become aggrieved when we see Heidi behaving liking Howard. Heidi violated our stereotypical expectations of women. The outcome: we like Howard, dislike Heidi.

Sandberg observes, "I have seen this dynamic play out over and over. When a woman excels at her job, both male and female

---

23   Deborah L. Rhode, *Women and Leadership* (New York: Oxford University Press, 2017), 10.

coworkers will remark that she may be accomplishing a lot but is 'not well-liked by her peers.' She is probably also 'too aggressive,'... or 'difficult.' At least, those are all things that have been said about me and almost every senior woman I know. The world seems to be asking why we can't be less like Heidi and more like Howard."[24] At this point, I almost feel like belting out the Henry Higgins *My Fair Lady* tune bemoaning why a woman can't be more like a man—but then if we are, we are dismissed and disliked.

Rather than swooning and wringing our hands over why there are so few women who ascend to—and further advance in—management and leadership roles, we need to pause and understand that a demonstrable bias against "strong" women is a critical component of why women are held back. And though there's been a paucity of research on women of color, emerging research finds similar trends for Juan and Juanita and Lakisha and Jamal too. Women, particularly women of color, are often thought to lack "executive presence."[25]

What is particularly disturbing is that this study was conducted a decade after the historic lawsuit filed by Ann Hopkins challenging these type of gender stereotypes (see Chapter Five). Yet, they persist. For women, even when we hold the same resumé and record of accomplishments, we are held to a different standard and regarded unfavorably. This holds true for *both* men and women judging Heidi. It's not just the men who are more likely to negatively perceive Heidi—it's women too. So much for the Sisterhood.

---

24   Sheryl Sandberg, *Lean In: Women, Work, and the Will to Lead* (New York: Alfred A. Knopf, 2013), 41.
25   Deborah L. Rhode, *Women and Leadership* (New York: Oxford University Press, 2017), 10.

Most of us have never heard of the Heidi-Howard study. Academic studies have largely been confined to professional trade publications, which few of us ever access or read. Because of the isolation of this research, most employers or human resource divisions—or the men and women they hire—have never heard of the study either. Because of stereotypical gender expectations, women find themselves in a "double bind": "damned if they do, damned if they don't" situations that carry over into all aspects of work and promotion from hiring, advancement, and salary compensation, to benefits, titles, and other perks.

Deborah L. Rhode's volume on *Women and Leadership* illustrates and outlines the body of research exposing this double-bind conundrum:[26] most of the traits that we attribute to people identified as leaders are those viewed as masculine, not feminine, such as dominance, authority, or assertiveness. While desirable in men, they are not deemed attractive in women. Though these views are

---

26   Deborah L. Rhode, *Women and Leadership* (New York: Oxford University Press, 2017), 10-15.

undergoing change, we are *still* much more ready to accept men as leaders. Individuals prefer a male to a female boss. Women are rated lower as leaders when they adopt authoritative styles. Female supervisors are disliked more than male supervisors for giving negative feedback, getting labeled as "bitch," "ice queen," and "iron maiden."

High-level female administrators report needing to work twice as hard and twice as good in order to just be viewed *equal* to men.[27] In one study of female university presidents, participants recounted how they are questioned on everything they do, and not taken as seriously as their male colleagues.[28] Says one, "I am still taken aback

---

27   Kelly Hannum, Shannon Muhly, Pamela Shockley-Zalabak, and Judith S. White, "Stories From the Summit Trail: Leadership Journeys of Senior Women in Higher Education," Higher Education Resource Services, August 2014, 16, https://hers-network.org/wp-content/uploads/2018/08/StoriesfromtheSummitTrail.pdf.

28   Kelly Hannum, Shannon Muhly, Pamela Shockley-Zalabak, and Judith S. White, "Stories From the Summit Trail: Leadership Journeys of Senior Women in Higher Education," Higher Education Resource Services, August 2014, 31, https://hers-network.org/wp-content/uploads/2018/08/StoriesfromtheSummitTrail.pdf.

by the level of…disrespect female administrators experience, behavior that male colleagues would not direct at male administrators."[29]

Carol Bartz, former chief of Autodesk and Yahoo, has described her industry as a "frat boy" environment. "They still gather together as males, excluding women from the inner circle."[30] This particularly impacts women of color. In my own career, I have seen the practice of male administrators not only allowing staff to bypass reporting to their female supervisor, but also engaging in back-channel communications with male members of the firm's board expressing their "concerns" over the female leader's competence. And these "old boys' club channels of communication" were allowed and encouraged to exist! Emily Chang describes a "Brotopia" in the technology world represented by California's Silicon Valley where men hold the cards and make the rules.[31]

These behaviors are not exactly random and are likely precursors for more nefarious future actions. Words matter. Attitudes matter. Indeed, studies provide systematic evidence "…that sexual harassment as traditionally defined for women—as consisting of sexual and sexist comments, unwanted sexual attention, and sexual coercion—is primarily targeted at women who step out of place by having masculine characteristics, or 'uppity' women. By implication, this suggests that sexual harassment is driven not out of desire for women who meet feminine ideals but out of a desire to punish those who violate

---

29   Linda Trinh Vo, "Navigating the Academic Terrain: The Racial and Gender Politics of Elusive Belonging," in *Presumed Incompetent: The Intersections of Race and Class for Women in Academia,* eds Gabriella Gutiérrez y Muhs, Yolanda Flores Niemann, Carmen G. González, and Angela P. Harris (Louisville, CO: University Press of Colorado, 2012), 93, 108.

30   Joann S. Lublin, *Earning It: Hard-Won Lessons From Trailblazing Women at the Top of the Business World* (New York: HarperCollins, 2016): 20.

31   Emily Chang, *Brotopia: Breaking Up the Boys' Club of Silicon Valley* (New York: Portfolio/Penguin, 2018).

them. In other words, it's not just about pejorative adjectives applied to 'strong' women but can lead to destructive behaviors as well."[32]

Rhodes describes an education summit wherein women were asked if they had ever been labeled as "bossy." Guess what? Every hand in the room was raised.[33] The discrepancy is not without notice: one university regent acknowledged that "if she were a [male university president], she would be regarded as an aggressive and strong leader, but as a woman, to many people she is a bitch."[34]

Data clearly shows that across a wide array of professions, women are seeking leadership posts, but while the number of women leaders has significantly increased, women continue to face an array of obstacles surrounding career advancement because of this thing we call "likability" in the workplace. We can break stereotypes, smash ceilings…but then we get caught up in a double bind that holds us back and punishes "strong" women.[35]

In 1986, two *Wall Street Journal* journalists, Carol Hymowitz and Timothy Schellhardt, introduced the "glass ceiling" metaphor and we've been bumping up against it ever since. They wrote: "Even those few women who rose steadily through the ranks eventually crashed into an invisible barrier. The executive suite seemed within their grasp, but they just couldn't break through the glass ceiling."[36] The image of a glass obstruction powerfully conveyed that women were being deluded about their opportunities because they could

---

32   Jennifer L. Berdahl, "The Sexual Harassment of Uppity Women," *Journal of Applied Psychology* 92, no. 2 (April 2007): 434, https://www.researchgate.net/publication/6436628_The_Sexual_Harassment_of_Uppity_Women.

33   Deborah L. Rhodes, *Women and Leadership* (New York: Oxford University Press, 2017), 99.

34   Mimi Wolverton, Beverly L. Bower, and Adrienne E. Hyle, *Women at the Top: What Women University and College Presidents Say About Effective Leadership* (Sterling, VA: Stylus, 2009), 61.

35   Dasie J. Schulz and Christine Enslin, "The Female Executive's Perspective on Experiences with Career Planning and Advancement in Organizations," *The Exchange* 3, no. 1 (July 2014): 57-67, https://papers.ssrn.com/sol3/papers.cfm?abstract_id=2526397.

36   Alice H. Eagly and Linda L. Carli, *Through the Labyrinth: The Truth About How Women Become Leaders* (Boston: Harvard Business School Press, 2007), 4.

not see their obstruction until they smashed right up against the transparent, invisible barrier (like a bird caught in a large dining hall surrounded by huge windows but no exit to freedom). Even the United States Congress recognized that the concept had galvanized the public, and a commission to investigate the glass ceiling was established, leading to conclusions that this type of discrimination stemmed from beliefs about women which had served to restrict their career advancement.

Decades later, a "think leader-think male perspective" continues to prevail, albeit women have made some progress. Female leaders, in particular, can be affected by a double-bind bias or the problem of a mismatch between what is expected of a leader and what is expected from a woman.

Most of us have heard of "Catch-22s," where no matter what you do, the outcome is not going to be pretty. The double bind is nothing short of women having to overcome competing and contradictory demands in leadership, behaviors, and performance.[37] Gendered stereotypes contribute to people's perceptions and expectations. Women are expected to be nurturing and consequently may come off as too soft when utilizing these attributes; on the other hand, if a woman is stern, assertive, and ambitious, she is conflicting with gender expectations. She's more likely to be labeled as tough. As many women leaders reveal, they need to be twice as good in order to just be evaluated as being on par with male colleagues, held to a higher performance standard than male leaders, even though they are compensated the same. Being a leader and being a female means

---

37   Dasie Schulz and Christine Enslin, "The Female Executive's Perspective on Career Planning and Advancement in Organizations: Experiences With Cascading Gender Bias, the Double-Bind, and Unwritten Rules to Advancement," *Sage Open* 4, no. 4 (November 2014): 1-9, https://www.researchgate.net/publication/285825358_The_Female_Executive's_Perspective_on_Career_Planning_and_Advancement_in_Organizations_Experiences_With_.

balancing passiveness and assertiveness only to satisfy the expectations of colleagues and other managers.

Researchers have found that there are two primary kinds of gender bias that affect women, labeled as descriptive and prescriptive bias. Descriptive gender stereotypes designate what women and men are like, and prescriptive gender stereotypes designate what women and men should be like.[38] Descriptive bias is the label we attach and associate with certain social groups and communities, and prescriptive bias is how they are expected to behave. And, when someone does not conform to these prescribed roles and behaviors, they can be penalized or punished. Women, for instance, are traditionally expected to be caring, warm, deferential, emotional, sensitive, and so on, and men are expected to be assertive, rational, competent, and objective. So, when it comes to promotion, these traits are sometimes automatically prescribed to people as per their gender without detailed information about their personalities; thereby a man, in general, is assumed to be a better fit as a leader.

The other side of this is prescriptive bias, when a woman who does not fit the role that is traditionally assigned to her and attempts to claim a traditionally male position is seen as breaking the norm. So, when a woman is decisive, she might be perceived as "brusque" and "abrupt." Therefore, for the same kind of leadership behavior, women might be penalized while men are commended.

This is the problem of "likability," where women who are not assertive and fit the gender stereotype of a woman as being gentle and caring are liked more but not considered as leadership material. On the other hand, women who display traditional "masculine" qual-

---

38   Madeline E. Heilman, "Gender stereotypes and workplace bias," *Research in Organizational Behavior* 32 (2012): 113-135, https://www.sciencedirect.com/science/article/abs/pii/S0191308512000093?via%3Dihub.

ities such as assertiveness, forcefulness, and ambition are labeled as "bitchy," unfeminine, and aggressive, and hence generally disliked. In both cases, women are then less likely to be promoted than men. Men do not face the same problem, because what is considered "bossy" in a woman is considered leadership skill in a man.

Female leaders are still thought to require an achievement-oriented aggressiveness and emotional toughness that is contrary to the stereotyped view of what women are like; as a result, the idea of a woman's success at a high-level position is unexpected. Expectations influence how information is processed; therefore, expectations produced by lack-of-fit perceptions can have important and broad-ranging consequences for how women are treated in the workplace. Bravo! When a man is successful, he can have it all. Both men and women like him. However, the case is not as rosy when a woman is successful. When she is successful, both men and women like her less. She's just not that *likable*.

What are these stereotypes that still bind women to days of the ancient past? The next chapter will more fully explore how we develop our views on gender based on our socialization and upbringing, but in a nutshell, researchers find that men and women are more likely to be defined with these attributes:

Men	**Women**
Providers	Caregivers
Decisive	Sensitive
Driven	Communal
Calm	Emotional
Direct	Indirect

We still seem to approach men and women with that proverbial perception that men and women are opposites—from Mars and Venus, remember? Because we still cling to this notion of "opposites," there is a stark polarity in how we view men's and women's professional achievements and traits associated with the binary. By focusing on Heidi's career and taking a calculated approach to amassing power, she was perceived as having violated our stereotypical expectations of women. Yet, by behaving in exactly the same style and manner, Howard lived up to our stereotypical expectations of men.

When we, as women, excel at our jobs, we may be accomplishing much but are not as well liked by our peers. The Heidis in the workplace are deemed "aggressive," "difficult," and so on. And those are the polite terms! But, given the stereotypes, this forces women into a "double-bind" dilemma. We're aware that when a woman acts forcefully or competitively, she's deviating from expected behavior. So, to get the job done, she "acts like a man" and then—even when she succeeds with outcomes—she pays the personal price and is disliked!

Research examining sex bias in work settings has shown that women are penalized for being successful in domains that are considered to be male and are disliked and interpersonally derogated as a consequence. Furthermore, research has shown that when a man helps out in the workplace, he is acknowledged and appreciated, and if he does not, it is not penalized. However, when a woman helps out, it is taken for granted, because that is her traditional role, and if she doesn't, she is considered mean and unhelpful, character traits that are not assigned to a leader.[39]

Women have to engage in a delicate dance in order to survive and thrive. Society typically raves over Fred Astaire as a great dancer. But Ginger Rogers had to do the exact thing—only backward, wearing heels, and avoiding tripping over those long ball gowns we all oohed and awed over!

Women experience a "backlash": as we've seen with Heidi, they are rated as equally competent to their male counterparts but

---

39   Madeline E. Heilman, "Gender stereotypes and workplace bias," *Research in Organizational Behavior* 32 (2012): 113-135, https://www.sciencedi-rect.com/science/article/abs/pii/S0191308512000093?via%3Dihub.

are perceived as much colder. Women who become managers in male-dominated fields are often the subject of intense negativity—employees tend to like and respect them less than male bosses. That's because when women act assertively or competitively, or when they appear emotionally restrained, these women are flouting gender norms about how they should behave. Researchers have found that this dislike comes from the perception that these women aren't nurturing or cooperative. The same research finds that when women *do* emphasize nurturing or interpersonal qualities, colleagues tend to like them more.

Social psychologists have found that most discriminatory behavior takes the form of implicit bias and results from gender schemas, the largely unexamined sets of ideas people hold concerning gender roles.[40] In one comprehensive analysis of sex discrimination, it was found that women's performance ratings exceed men's in jobs that are sex-typed female but suffer when compared with men in jobs perceived as "male."[41]

So, "leading" like a woman has particular limitations, forcing women to have to choose: do you want to be respected but not liked, or liked but not respected? In a definitive examination of women and leadership, author Deborah L. Rhode argues that, essentially,

40　Virginia Valian, *Why So Slow? The Advancement of Women* (Cambridge, MA: MIT Press, 1998); Mahzarin R. Banaji and Anthony G. Greenwald, "Implicit Gender Stereotyping in Judgments of Fame," *Journal of Personality and Social Psychology* 68, no. 2 (1995): 181-198, https://faculty.washington.edu/agg/pdf/Banaji_Gwald_JPSP_1995.OCR.pdf;

Monica Biernat and Elizabeth R. Thompson, "Shifting Standards and Contextual Variation in Stereotyping," *European Review of Social Psychology* 12 (2002): 103-137, https://www.tandfonline.com/doi/abs/10.1080/14792772143000030; Laurie A. Rudman and Peter Glick, "Prescriptive Gender Stereotypes and Backlash Toward Agentic Women," *Journal of Social Issues* 57, no. 4 (2001): 743-762, https://spssi.onlinelibrary.wiley.com/doi/abs/10.1111/0022-4537.00239.

41　Heather K. Davison and Michael J. Burke, "Sex Discrimination in Simulated Employment Contexts: A Meta-analytic Investigation," *Journal of Vocational Behavior* 56 (2000): 225-248, https://eric.ed.gov/?id=EJ602854.

"…women face trade-offs that men do not…."[42] Underlying the skewed representation and paucity of women in leadership positions are societal and culturally sanctioned attitudinal differences in the expectation and evaluation of male and female leadership. Both men and women hold more negative attitudes toward female than toward male authorities. Some research has uncovered that we will tolerate and sanction leadership when it occurs in gender-congruent roles, i.e., when we expect a woman to be in charge.[43] Owning one's success is key to achieving more success. But women taking credit also comes at a social and professional cost. A woman who explains why she is qualified or mentions previous successes in a job interview can lower her chances of getting hired.

In other words, when we walk into a workplace, we are entering established institutions with historical practices, cultures, norms, rules, and patterns of discrimination against women and minority group members in hiring and evaluation, especially in traditional male fields.[44] And women, even when producing identical work product, are not only held to higher standards than men,[45] but are more likely to be demeaned. Indeed, in one research study, several groups were asked to evaluate the work of male and female authors who wrote identical articles. One group was composed of all men, another all women, and the final, a mix of men and women. The

---

42   Deborah L. Rhode, *Women and Leadership* (New York: Oxford University Press, 2017), 12.

43   Alice H. Eagly and Mary C. Johannesen-Schmidt, "The Leadership Styles of Women and Men," *Journal of Social Issues* 57, no. 4 (2001): 781-797, https://spssi.onlinelibrary.wiley.com/doi/abs/10.1111/0022-4537.00241.

44   Veronica F. Nieva and Barbara A. Gutek, "Sex Effects on Evaluation," *Academy of Management Review* 5, no. 2 (April 1980): 267-276, https://www.jstor.org/stable/257436?seq=1; Madeline E. Heilman, Aaron S. Wallen, Daniella Fuchs, and Melinda, M. Tamkins, "Penalties for Success: Reactions to Women Who Succeed at Male Gender-Typed Tasks," *Journal of Applied Psychology* 89, no. 3 (2004): 416-427, https://psycnet.apa.org/record/2004-95165-003; Marianne Bertrand and Sendhil Mullianathan, "Are Emily and Greg More Employable Than Lakisha and Jamal? A Field Experiment on Labor Market Discrimination," *American Economic Review* 94, no. 4 (September 2004): 991-1013, https://www.aeaweb.org/articles?id=10.1257/0002828042002561.

45   Deborah L. Rhode, *Women and Leadership* (New York: Oxford University Press, 2017).

study concluded that in the presence of men, "both men and women devalued the female-authored articles" while women accorded men greater recognition and "preferential treatment." The preferential treatment included "downgrading women, women's accomplishments, and the importance of interacting with women."[46] The degradation of male achievements or leadership, however, is unlikely to occur. I was once "written up" because I had spoken three minutes longer than a male colleague in a meeting. Not only was I not wearing pink that day, but I suppose I was not being properly deferential to his outsized ego. Months later, I was told by concerned former colleagues that key male executives had actually gone out of their way (but always behind my back) to question and undermine my leadership skills.

Although focused on women in academic science and engineering, the National Academy of Sciences, National Academy of Engineering, and National Academy of Medicine highlight the role of gender bias and discrimination in how women are perceived, judged, and evaluated.[47] Gender bias has largely been unexamined, but it has played a major role in limiting women's opportunities and stalling career advancements because of how we think about stereotypical career paths, which negatively impacts women and ethnic minorities.

What is somewhat ironic is that, under affirmative action programs, white women have often been identified as benefiting from preferential treatment. Yet, these studies indicate that the preferential treatment continues to seemingly operate in favor of

---

46   Nancy L. Toder, "The Effect of the Sexual Composition of a Group on Discrimination Against Women and Sex-Role Attitudes," *Psychology of Women Quarterly*, first published Dec. 1, 1980, https://journals.sagepub.com/doi/10.1111/j.1471-6402.1980.tb00963.x.

47   National Academy of Sciences, National Academy of Engineering, and National Academy of Medicine, "Success and Its Evaluation in Science and Engineering," in *Beyond Bias and Barriers: Fulfilling the Potential of Women in Academic Science and Engineering*, (National Academies Press, 2007).

men. Indeed, "under a hostile form of gender bias, women who aspire to traditionally masculine roles are seen as undermining or attacking the rightful prerogatives of men. The combination of those biases often causes competent women to be perceived as 'not nice' or even 'overly aggressive' and traditionally subservient women to be perceived as 'incompetent' and 'trivial.'"[48]

In studies where a man is seated at the head of a table, observers are likely to presume him to be a leader, but do not ascribe the same attribution when it is a female occupying that chair.[49] Ever been on jury duty? A study on jurors' participation during deliberation uncovered disadvantages women face in being recognized as leaders. Men are typically selected as the foreperson or presiding juror on a jury and have significantly higher participation rates during deliberation compared to women, making it difficult for women to shape the jury's deliberations.[50] Disturbingly, women's contributions appear to be diminished at the workplace—and even on jury duty!

So, congratulations: you've broken the glass ceiling and entered a workplace historically not as accessible to women as to men. But once seated in that coveted Executive Suite, should women have to contend with a culture that has not kept up with the pace of women crashing through those ceilings and a host of attitudes and biases that subject them to encounter an "unfit for leadership" judgment? "Of course not!" should be our response. But, in fact, the National Academy of Sciences, National Academy of Engineering, and National

48   Peter Glick and Susan T. Fiske, "The Ambivalent Sexism Inventory: Differentiating Hostile and Benevolent Sexism," *Journal of Personality and Social Psychology* 70, no. 3 (March 1996): 491-512, https://psycnet.apa.org/record/1996-03014-006.
49   Virginia Valian, "The Cognitive Bases of Gender Bias," *Brooklyn Law Review* 65, (1999): 1048-49. (Originally found here: https://brooklynworks.brooklaw.edu/blr/vol65/iss4/3/.
50   Erin York Cornwell and Valerie P. Hans, "Contextualizing Jury Participation: Case-, Jury-, and Juror-Level Predictors of Participation in Jury Deliberations," Cornell University, posted Aug. 2, 2009, https://papers.ssrn.com/sol3/papers.cfm?abstract_id=1441537."

Academy of Medicine, finds that this is precisely what is expected in the traditionally male-dominated fields of science and research they studied, concluding that stereotyping and cognitive bias have created "built-in headwinds" for women and minorities in science and engineering. Hence, they warn, "one of the conclusions, then, is that that person is viewed as not 'one of us,' is less collegial, and is not promoted at a comparable pace as others."[51] But it's not just from the hard sciences that women have been historically denied entrance. It exists across domains.

Women in leadership confront a double bind with contradictory demands for performance, behavior, and leadership.[52] Because the demands are conflicting, there really is no easy pathway out: that damned "damned if you do, damned if you don't" begins to resemble a dreaded Sophie's choice impacting women. Hence, the conflicting demands require women to demonstrate contradictory behaviors that set them up for harsh judgment no matter which behavior is adopted and forces women to choose between equally unsatisfactory alternatives.[53] If a female leader is assertive and firm (not nurturing or compassionate), that woman will be labeled too tough, yet still be expected to deliver to higher standards than her male counterparts. Women are required to prove leadership ability repeatedly, and when they must perform more consistently and at a higher level than male counterparts, they receive the same or lower

---

51   National Academy of Sciences, National Academy of Engineering, and National Academy of Medicine, "Success and Its Evaluation in Science and Engineering," in *Beyond Bias and Barriers: Fulfilling the Potential of Women in Academic Science and Engineering*, (National Academies Press, 2007): 2-153.

52   "Report: 2007 Catalyst Census of Women Board Directors of the Fortune 500," Catalyst, posted December 10, 2007, https://www.catalyst.org/research/2007-catalyst-census-of-women-board-directors-of-the-fortune-500/.

53   "Report: 2007 Catalyst Census of Women Board Directors of the Fortune 500," Catalyst, posted December 10, 2007, https://www.catalyst.org/research/2007-catalyst-census-of-women-board-directors-of-the-fortune-500/.

compensation, recognition, or opportunities. In my career I have heard women described as "bitching" and "moaning" when giving critical feedback to a male executive's presentation. Of course, male executives don't do that, right? They "critique" and "amplify" and "clarify." *Whatever.*

The predicament described as competent but disliked spotlights how female managers and executives are challenged with balancing passiveness with assertiveness to satisfy the expectations of colleagues and managers. Regardless of experience, performance results, ability, influence, or use of power, female managers must endure constant scrutiny and judgment from others who inevitably label them as too soft or too hard. Competent but disliked is a predicament that describes the dilemma of being seen either as someone who takes charge or someone who takes care.

The result is that female leaders are perceived as likable or competent, but rarely both. We just don't really *like* our female bosses, and many of us still prefer to work for a male.[54] Hollywood helps promote and perpetuate the dislike: after all, who can erase the ruthless image and tone of Miranda Priestly as the devilish Prada-wearing boss who terrorizes her staff? And following the success of the she-devil boss, Hollywood has spun off television series with similar characters zipped tightly into pencil skirts caricatures.[55]

---

54   Deborah L. Rhode, *Women and Leadership* (Oxford University Press: New York, 2017), 10; Alice H. Eagly and Linda L. Carli, *Through the Labyrinth: The Truth About How Women Become Leaders* (Boston: Harvard Business School Press, 2007), 97.

55   Alyssa Rosenberg, "How 'The Devil Wears Prada' foreshadowed an age of antiheroines," *The Washington Post,* June 30, 2016, https://www.washingtonpost.com/news/act-four/wp/2016/06/30/how-the-devil-wears-prada-foreshadowed-an-age-of-antiheroines/.

THE RESISTANCE IS REAL: DON'T PASS GO, DON'T GET OUT OF JAIL FREE: THE PRICE ALL WOMEN PAY FOR GENDER BIAS

There's a price that all women pay for gender, for being female, whether one realizes this or not.

The resistance to women's leadership has been documented in academic research, as well as, increasingly, in court cases brought by women in the workforce who have been willing to stand up and demand an end to gender bias. Though it's a new field of research, already more than a handful of studies show that people associate women and men with different traits. Unfortunately, we still link men with more of the traits that connote leadership. This sets up a clash of what psychologists call "communal" and "agentic." Women are associated with the communal qualities, which convey a concern for the compassionate treatment of others, including being affectionate, helpful, friendly, kind, sympathetic, interpersonally sensitive, gentle, soft-spoken. On the other hand, men are associated with agentic qualities, which convey assertion and control. These qualities include being aggressive, ambitious, dominant, self-confident, forceful, self-reliant, individualistic.

Unfortunately, in studies in which we evaluate qualities needed for leaders, we associate agentic traits with effective leadership. Not surprisingly, this may be due to a long history of males in leadership roles, and it is hard to separate the leader from male associations.

Hence, female leaders find themselves in a quandary once again. If women are highly communal, they may be criticized for not being agentic enough. But if they are highly agentic, they may be criticized for lacking empathy. Either way, they don't have "the right stuff" for powerful jobs. They are, in the words that I was called, "a mismatch" and susceptible to criticism, a poor evaluation, a stalled career advancement, or even termination.

Overall, people are more resistant to women's influence than men's. Studies have examined reactions to men and women engaging in various types of dominant behavior, producing fairly consistent findings. Nonverbal dominance, such as staring at others while speaking to them or pointing at people, is a more damaging behavior for women than for men. Hence, do we like women more when they avert their eyes, look downwards? Interestingly, these are behaviors typically associated with fear and subservience.

Verbally intimidating others can undermine a woman's influence, and assertive behavior can reduce her chances of winning a job or advancing in her career. Simply disagreeing can sometimes get women into trouble. Men who disagree or otherwise act dominant are more likely to be accepted. Not so much for women.

So, despite climbing and battling yourself to gain access to the coveted C-suite, are we supposed to behave as sugar and spice and everything nice? Ironically, when women are "nice," there is no credit for it: they are just *expected* to be nice. Nice behavior that seems noteworthy in men seems unimpressive in women. Men have more freedom. People like men equally well and are equally influenced by them regardless of their warmth. Female supervisors are disliked more than male supervisors for giving the same negative feedback.[56] A 2005 Catalyst study of gender stereotyping and leadership found that top managers reporting to women supervisors have a more, not less, stereotypical view of women leaders than those who reported

56   Peter Glick & Susan T. Fiske, "Sex Discrimination: The Psychological Approach," in *Sex Discrimination in the Workplace: Multidisciplinary Perspectives*, ed. Faye J. Crosby, Margaret S. Stockdale, and Ann S. Ropp (Malden, MA: Blackwell, 2007), 155, 173.

to men, and respondents reporting to women in male-dominated fields are more critical of women leaders than those working in fields identified as more feminine.[57] Women find themselves in double jeopardy. In masculine domains, individuals who report to women may have the least confidence in women's problem-solving competence. This means women's subordinates—the very team members she is turning toward to get work done—are the very people who may have the lowest confidence in their plans.

Quite frankly, research shows that male or female, we don't like female bosses! It all amounts to a clash of assumptions when we experience or confront a woman in management, and simply hiring more women without addressing pervasive, persistent stereotypes has not erased discriminatory outcomes.

At that point, the labels flood in: deceitful, pushy, selfish, abrasive. Male counterparts, not so much. People suspect that such highly effective women must not be very likable or nice; rather than improving, we may be going backward. In fact, sociologist and lead researcher for Sheryl Sandberg's groundbreaking book, *Lean In: Women, Work and the Will to Lead*, Marianne Cooper rejects the conclusion that things are getting better for women,[58] and that "likeability and success actually go together remarkably well for women" in their designed leadership programs.[59]

Rather, Cooper's work and the continuing research in this area consistently reveal that, disturbingly, for women leaders, likability

---

57 "Women 'Take Care,' Men 'Take Charge' - Stereotyping of U.S. Business Leaders Exposed," Catalyst, posted October 19, 2005, 24, https://www.catalyst.org/research/women-take-care-men-take-charge-stereotyping-of-u-s-business-leaders-exposed/.

58 Marianne Cooper, "For Women Leaders, Likability and Success Hardly Go Hand-in-Hand," *Harvard Business Review*, April 30, 2013, https://hbr.org/2013/04/for-women-leaders-likability-a.

59 Jack Zenger and Joseph Folkman," New Research Shows Success Doesn't Make Women Likeable," blog post, quoted in Marianne Cooper, *Harvard Business Review*, April 30, 2013, https://hbr.org/2013/04/for-women-leaders-likability-a.

and success hardly go hand-in-hand, pointing out methodological flaws in the measurement of such. Scoffs Cooper, "As a sociologist who focuses on gender, work, and family it is always nice for me to hear when things are going well for women at work. I mean wouldn't it be great if this one analysis could disprove decades of social science research—by psychologists like Madeline Heilman at New York University, Laurie Rudman at Rutgers, Peter Glick at Lawrence University, and Amy Cuddy at Harvard."[60]

She points out the whiplash message with which highly successful women live: they may be applauded for successful outcomes, but then find themselves being told to change who they are—reprimanded for being "too aggressive," "out for herself," "difficult," and "abrasive." Cooper reminds us of Jill Abramson, the first woman executive editor of the *New York Times*. Yet, she was ousted after confronting the top brass on, reportedly, discrepancies in issues pertaining to pay and pensions. She was described by staffers as "impossible to work with," and "not approachable," just days after the paper won four Pulitzer Prizes (the third highest number ever received by the newspaper).[61] To win a Pulitzer Prize in journalism is the highest award. Yet, even with that record of success, she was still shown the door. The management's narrative that she was "pushy" is a characterization that has an inescapably gendered aspect applied to women.

The social science research on success-likability punishments clearly tells us that women and men can be viewed as similarly competent, yet still receive different likability scores. Scientific research also tells us that female leaders are disliked much more

---

60   Marianne Cooper, "For Women Leaders, Likability and Success Hardly Go Hand-in-Hand," *Harvard Business Review*, April 30, 2013, https://hbr.org/2013/04/for-women-leaders-likability-a.

61   Dylan Byers, "Turbulence at The Times," *Politico*. April 23, 2013.

than men when acting authoritatively. To be clear, it is not that women are always disliked more than men when they are successful, but they are often penalized when they behave in ways that violate gender stereotypes. High-achieving women experience social backlash because their very success—and specifically the behaviors that created that success—violates our expectations about how women are supposed to behave. Women are expected to be nice, warm, friendly, and nurturing. Thus, if a woman acts assertively or competitively, if she pushes her team to perform, if she exhibits decisive and forceful leadership, she is deviating from the social script that dictates how she "should" behave.

Posits Cooper, "By violating beliefs about what women are like, successful women elicit pushback from others for being insufficiently feminine and too masculine. As descriptions like 'Ice Queen,' and 'Ballbuster' can attest, we are deeply uncomfortable with powerful women. In fact, we often don't really like them."[62] She notes that some rosy depictions about the correlation between gender and likability ignore the scientific evidence which consistently finds that men and women doing the same thing are evaluated differently. She concludes, "If Jill Abramson were John Abramson, we would likely be having a different conversation."[63]

It is important to be right about these things. Getting it wrong only obscures the real penalties women pay (i.e., not getting promoted, or being ousted) for simply doing what they need to do, and what men are allowed to do, in order to get to the top. Little

62   Marianne Cooper, "For Women Leaders, Likability and Success Hardly Go Hand-in-Hand," *Harvard Business Review*, April 30, 2013, https://hbr.org/2013/04/for-women-leaders-likability-a.

63   Marianne Cooper, "For Women Leaders, Likability and Success Hardly Go Hand-in-Hand," *Harvard Business Review*, April 30, 2013, https://hbr.org/2013/04/for-women-leaders-likability-a.

girls (and little boys for that matter) would be better served by an informed conversation about gender stereotypes and how biased ways of thinking hinder career success.

But do women have to change themselves in order to fit gender stereotypes?

If all things were equal, one might think that leaders should just act like leaders with strong agentic characteristics. One might think that if women were to demonstrate more agentic characteristics and start to "act" more like a traditional leader, they would be more accepted in the role. But as we know, that's not the case. Women who demonstrate agentic leadership behaviors are penalized for acting against the traditional female gender role. As such, it often leads to agentic female leaders being unliked and unpopular. She's damned if she does, and damned if she doesn't. *What's a girl to do?* If she acts like a leader, she will be disliked. If she stereotypically acts like a woman should, she won't be seen as a leader. Call it a double bind, a Catch-22, or just a bitch—the bias is real.

Kim Scott, author of the book *Radical Candor: How to Get What You Want by Saying What You Mean*, shares her experience with her readers, writing,

"One day my boss called me into his office and asked if I was familiar with the research about the relationship between women's competence vs likeability in the workplace. I wasn't and he explained point-blank that the more competent a woman is, the less her colleagues tend to like her. There were a couple of people I worked with who, perhaps because of gender bias, simply didn't like me, my boss said. Rather than asking these people to re-evaluate their attitudes, he asked me to work on my 'likeability.'

Naturally, I thought he should address the gender bias, not tell me to work around it by baking cookies for people who resented my competence.... I knew I could be obnoxiously aggressive sometimes; I don't know anyone in a leadership position who doesn't fall into that quadrant a little more often than they'd like to.... My boss called me into his office once more. He said things were better, but he had an idea that would totally put the issue to rest. I was all ears. His suggestion? A demotion for me. That way, he explained, my colleague would not be so jealous of my position. That would make it easier for me to be more 'likeable.' Less than three weeks later, I found another, better job and quit."[64]

Kieran Snyder, cofounder of Textio, applied linguistic analysis to performance reviews and found that when women challenge directly—which they must do to be successful—they get penalized for being "abrasive," a label that not only is used quite a bit, but gets placed on women by other women as well as by men. She detailed her findings for *Fortune* magazine, to which many women responded.[65]

Writes Scott, "Why did this article strike such a nerve? Every professional woman I know has many, many stories of being called abrasive, or of being disliked for being too competent—and of paying the price emotionally and professionally."[66] For women to succeed, performance reviews are critical, and each one affects future promotions and opportunities for career advancement. The impact on

---

64   Kim Scott, "The Price All Women Pay for Gender Bias," Women@Forbes, posted January 31, 2018, https://www.forbes.com/sites/break-the-future/2018/01/31/why-gender-bias-holds-us-all-back/?sh=677eb25b4c5f.

65   Kieran Snyder, "The abrasiveness trap: High-achieving men and women are described differently in reviews," *Fortune*, August 26, 2014.

66   Kim Scott, "The Price All Women Pay for Gender Bias," Women@Forbes, posted January 31, 2018, https://www.forbes.com/sites/break-the-future/2018/01/31/why-gender-bias-holds-us-all-back/?sh=677eb25b4c5f.

female leadership is profound. Scott outlines the negative career impacts by identifying what happens to promotions over the course of several years when bias impacts ratings just a little bit.[67] When gender bias accounts for just 5 percent of the difference in performance ratings, an organization that starts out with 58 percent of the entry-level positions filled by women winds up with only 29 percent of the leadership positions filled by women.

But the double bind exacerbates the disparity. When women are thought of as "abrasive" they tend to fall behind their male counterparts. Snyder refers to this as a "lost generation," which means less income for women and their families and a world where women are shut out of leadership positions that are (and remain) overwhelmingly male. If a woman is early enough in her career, she'll probably get promoted eventually despite her alleged "abrasiveness," but now she's a year or so "behind." Fast-forward another five to seven years. Now her male colleagues are two levels ahead of her. Since pay increases steeply with each promotion, he's now getting paid a lot more than she is. When she gets married and has a child, guess whose career is more important for family income, and who's more likely to stay home from work when the baby is sick? She is.

But that's not even the worst-case scenario. Let's imagine that she takes the "abrasive" feedback to heart and quits challenging her reports directly. She adjusts her behavior so that she's more likable but less effective at work. So now, in addition to gender bias, there are real performance issues to contend with. In this case, she's never going to get ahead. Frustrated beyond measure and feeling that she

---

67   Kim Scott, "The Price All Women Pay for Gender Bias," Women@Forbes, posted January 31, 2018, https://www.forbes.com/sites/break-the-future/2018/01/31/why-gender-bias-holds-us-all-back/?sh=677eb25b4c5f.

must choose between being liked and being successful, she decides that this is not a game worth playing and quits.

Or gets fired.

It may be dangerous to succeed in a gender-atypical occupation. Women who are acknowledged to have been personally successful in a masculine gender-typed job run a real risk of being disliked—and being disliked can have a negative effect on one's career.[68]

And once it starts, the consequences can be quite insidious for all women, because practices that equate leadership with behaviors considered more common and acceptable for men suggest that beyond likability, women are simply not cut out to be leaders.

Even absent the lack of discriminatory intent, these subtle "second generation" forms of workplace gender bias can lead to an underrepresentation of women in top positions.

All the "You go, girl" cheers simply are reduced to an unconscious reinforcement of entrenched beliefs that serve to maintain and perpetuate old boys' clubs and the status quo.

As leaders, we influence. And quite frankly, all that power really is the ability to influence. Paula Johnson, a pioneer in research on gender and power, suggests that there are three major dimensions on which the use of power to exert influence is affected by gender stereotypes: directness, concreteness, and competence. According to her analysis, gender norms dictate that men's influence styles can be direct, concrete, and competent, but women's should be indirect, personal, and based on helplessness or dependence.[69]

68   Madeline Heilman, Aaron S. Wallen, Daniella Fuchs, and Melinda M. Tamkins, "Penalties For Success: Reactions to Women Who Succeed at Male Gender-Typed Tasks," *Journal of Applied Psychology* 89, no. 3 (2004): 416-427.

69   Paula Johnson, "Women and Power: Toward a Theory of Effectiveness," *Journal of Social Issues* 32, no. 3 (1976): 99-110.

Recall that old adage: in order to "catch a man," let him think it was *his* idea. And if that doesn't work, then cook up a hearty meal because the way to a man's heart is through his stomach.

Well, that is a form of influence, but it's not direct. Direct influence is demonstrated when a person uses power openly, by giving an order or making a request. Indirect influence is exercised when the individual obtains the desired outcome while trying to keep the other person unaware of the influence. Indirect influence is often called "manipulation." There are still many constraints against directness by women and, consequently, women more than men tend to rely on indirect influence. A woman who uses direct power is quickly labeled "unfeminine," "castrating," and "bitchy." Popular women's magazines often encourage readers to use manipulative rather than direct strategies to get what they want. ("Let him think it was his idea.")[70]

Men and women are *expected* to use power in different ways. In one research study, respondents were given a list of fifteen different methods of influence that could be used in a given hypothetical situation and then asked to identify if it was a male or female employing that influence strategy. The study results showed that, indeed, respondents expected certain strategies to be used more by men than by women, including direct use of informational power. Men are allowed to use many different forms of influence, depending on the situation, but women are more severely restricted to the less aggressive types. Since then, many researchers have documented that people do expect women and men to base their influence on different resources.[71] Other studies also show that males are more

---

70   Hilary M. Lips, *Sex & Gender: An Introduction,* 7th ed.
        (Long Grove, IL: Waveland Press, 2020), 508.
71   Paula Johnson, "Women and Power: Toward a Theory of Effective-
        ness," *Journal of Social Issues* 32, no. 3 (1976): 99-110.

likely to use direct, assertive strategies, whereas females are more likely to use indirect, submissive ones."[72]

The studies continue to pile up: a 2018 study of 1,150 participants found people were less likely to refer a female to a job opening when the description emphasized intellectual ability. In fact, when a job description mentioned "brilliance," participants were 25.3 percent less likely to recommend a woman for the role versus when that word was left out.[73]

A 2019 study showed similar results.[74] The study's authors looked at 24,000 scientific grant applications to see how men and women were funded for their respective research. The authors found that when the scientific ideas were evaluated, men and women were equally likely to receive a grant. But when the promise or talent of the scientist was considered, men were 1.4 times as likely to receive the money. And while the problem is systemic, acknowledgement of it isn't necessarily objective. According to a University of Cambridge study of nearly 6,000 employees in the United Kingdom, around 74 percent of female workers surveyed said their workplace culture presented barriers to advancement for women. Some 53 percent of women reported seeing female colleagues judged more negatively than their male peers. And just 18 percent of men noticed the same thing.[75]

---

72   Hilary M. Lips, *Sex & Gender: An Introduction,* 7th ed. (Long Grove, IL: Waveland Press, 2020), 510.

73   "Evidence of Bias Against Girls and Women in Contexts that Emphasize Intellectual Clarity," *OSFHome.* July 7, 2017.

74   Jennifer L. Raymond and Miriam B. Goodman, "Funders Should Evaluate Projects, Not People," *The Lancet*, February 9, 2019, https://www.thelancet.com/journals/lancet/article/PIIS0140-6736(19)30280-6/fulltext#articleInformation.

75   Jill Armstrong and Jason Ghaboos, "Gender Bias in Workplace Culture Curbs Careers," Murray Edwards College, February 2019, https://www.murrayedwards.cam.ac.uk/sites/default/files/files/CWM%20Gender%20Bias%20REPORT%20FINAL%2020190211.pdf.

HELLO....IT'S NOT JUST THE CEILING, BUT THE ENTIRE ORGANIZATIONAL STRUCTURE AND FOUNDATION

Hence, what confronts women in their professional endeavors is not just a need to smash the proverbial glass ceilings. It's more entrenched, challenging, and complex than that. Researchers Alice Eagly and Linda Carli deem these double binds and double standards as a "labyrinth" that needs to be carefully navigated. A labyrinth—rather than a single ceiling—conveys the idea of a complex journey toward a goal worth striving for. Passage isn't simple or direct, but it requires persistence and awareness of one's progress. Routes are full of twists and turns. And unlike Dorothy who was given ruby red slippers to navigate her road to Oz, no such magic shoes exist for women today.

Stereotypes of women leaders isn't anything new. In 2007, journalist Shankar Vedantam cataloged the derogatory descriptions of some of the first female world leaders:[76]

- England's Margaret Thatcher: Attila the Hen;

- Golda Meir, Israel's first female prime minister: the only man in the Cabinet;

- Indira Gandhi, India's first female prime minister: the old witch;

- Angela Merkel, German chancellor: the Iron Frau.

We can add to his catalog with virtually the same descriptors in modern times:

- 2020 U.S. presidential candidates Senator Elizabeth Warren and Senator Amy Klobuchar were called "angry women"; on the other hand, U.S. presidential candidate Bernie Sanders—who seemed to always be yelling—was more fondly embraced.

- 2016 U.S. presidential candidate Hillary Clinton was called a "nasty woman."

- 2020 U.S. Vice President Kamala Harris (while a candidate) was called "a nasty woman."

- Retired U.S. Senator Barbara Boxer was criticized for asking to be called Senator, not "Ma'am."

- I was called "bombastic" as a California senator and majority leader.

---

76   Shankar Vedantam, "'Nicer Sex' Image at Play in Politics," *Chicago Tribune*, November 13, 2007, http://articles.chicagotribune.com/2007-11-13/news/0711120690_1_female-leaders-women-and-leadership-social-psychologist.

Irrespective of how one feels about women who have run for the U.S. presidency, almost all have been labeled "unlikable," including former secretary of state and Senator Hillary Clinton, Senator Elizabeth Warren, and Vice President Kamala Harris, also a former senator. In fact, the Republican leader and representative of California's 23rd district in the House of Representatives tweeted out, "as my daughter told me after watching last night's #VPdebate: 'Kamala almost makes Hillary Clinton likable.'" Of course, I replied with a tweet of my own urging us to judge all women candidates on their records—not their likability. As we know, women deemed strong are automatically at a disadvantage. For days following the vice-presidential debate between Senator Harris and Vice President Mike Pence, social media was aflutter with questions about whether women in politics can ever be "likable" to the voters.

And, oh: women also have to worry about how we look while doing the job—from how much cleavage is exposed, to monotone pantsuits, to how our hair is coiffed, to what shoes we wear.

But remember *The Wolf of Wall Street*? Not only did leading actor Leonardo DiCaprio play the archetypal Wall Street CEO who does drugs, drinks, womanizes (I'd call it sexual harassment), breaks the law, hires hookers, cheats on his spouse, and degrades males and females, but he is depicted as a hero to all tough men in New York and to audiences everywhere, and we *like* him! Not only was it a major commercial success, grossing $392 million worldwide during its theatrical run and becoming Director Martin Scorsese's highest-grossing film, but it was nominated for several Academy Awards.

Can you imagine the female equivalent of him? NO WAY!

Dr. Pragya Agarwal, an inclusivity consultant, behavioral scientist, speaker, and author, points out that the research clearly shows that unconscious bias is rife in the workplace. Gender stereotypes, in particular, are everywhere. It is in the language that we use, and it is the way we perceive women in the workplace.[77] It's even how we *laugh*, as presidential candidate Hillary Clinton soon discovered when she campaigned for the presidency in 2008. Some commentators made references to her being a bitch.[78] Journalists seemed preoccupied with her laugh, calling it a "cackle," a word associated with witches.[79] Comedian Jon Stewart skewered her with a compilation of her outbursts on his weekly show, concluding, "She'll be our first president that you can't spill water on." It's also how we move: in my career, I have been told that I don't keep my arms and hands pinned to my side at all times and "use my hands" when I speak and stand. Golly gee. I suppose if I were corseted into a straightjacket and not allowed any freedom of movement, I would be less "intimidating"?

Whether politics or executive suites, women who lead confront gender stereotypes and double "likability" standards.

But how did we get here? How did we learn to become Heidi or Howard in the first place, and what needs to be done to change this? Chapter Three will review how we learned these cultural standards of sugar and spice and everything nice that we teach to little Heidi, but that haunts her when she seeks to lead.

---

77 Pragya Agarwal, "Here is Why Organisations Need to Be Conscious of Unconscious Bias," *Forbes*, August 26, 2018, https://www.forbes.com/sites/pragyaagarwaleurope/2018/08/26/here-is-why-organisations-need-to-be-conscious-of-unconscious-bias/?sh=5eb423a726b2.

78 Susan J. Carroll, "Reflections on Gender and Hillary Clinton's Presidential Campaign: The Good, the Bad, and the Misogynic," *Politics & Gender* 5, no. 1 (Cambridge: Cambridge University Press, March 9, 2009): 1-20. See also Jennifer L. Lawless, "Sexism and Gender Bias in Election 2008: A More Complex Path for Women in Politics," *Politics & Gender* 5, no. 1 (Cambridge: Cambridge University Press, March 9, 2009): 70-80.

79 Patrick Healy, "The Clinton Conundrum: What's Behind the Laugh?" *New York Times*, September 30, 2007, https://www.nytimes.com/2007/09/30/us/politics/30clinton.html.

CHAPTER THREE

Sugar 'n Spice and Everything Nice: "Would you like the Girl Toy or the Boy Toy with your Happy Meal?"

Once upon a time, my daughter and I pulled up at McDonald's to order a Happy Meal. As a single mom, I just did not have the time or the wherewithal to cook. Leaving the university, we entered the drive-through lane at our neighborhood McDonald's and the voice crackled through the microphone, taking our order. Then the question was asked—the one that has followed every little boy or girl from infancy, through childhood, and to infinity and beyond:

"Would you like the girl toy or the boy toy with your Happy Meal?"

I just responded that we were here for the cheeseburger but asked what the toys were so that my daughter could choose.

Clearly, my response back to the microphone did not compute, and the voice came back insisting that I identify the boy or girl toy based on if it was a boy or girl child.

Ok, I admit it: I had just finished a long day lecturing at the university on sex and gender and prejudice and discrimination and had not expected to have to engage in another lecture via a drive-through restaurant. What difference does the sex of my child make, I asked; can you just tell me what the toys are so my child can state her preference?

Aha, the employee responded, it's a girl, she will get the doll. Now I wasn't ready to let this go. Why?, I asked. That's stereotyping and forcing dolls down the throats of all little girls who drive through this fast-food lane in search of a cheeseburger Happy Meal! Why can't she just choose? She might want the so-called boy toy. What is the other choice?

There is none, the voice crackled through the microphone. Girls get dolls, boys get cars. The employee in charge of Happy Meal orders wouldn't tell me, and whether we liked it or not, a pink plastic miniature doll would accompany what was becoming a not-so-happy cheeseburger meal experience that day. Ultimately, we pulled out of line in the fast lane, went inside to the counter, and walked out with my daughter's choice and a not-so-happy meal.

Although dramatic changes have occurred over the past century in our concepts of masculinity and femininity and the rights accorded women, one thing has changed very little: almost universally the male-female distinction has been ascribed meaning and roles that have impacted virtually all aspects of our social life.[80]

---

80   Hilary M. Lips, *Sex & Gender: An Introduction,* 7th ed. (Long Grove, IL: Waveland Press, 2020).

As Hilary M. Lips identifies, "…Sex stereotypes are socially shared beliefs about what qualities can be assigned to individuals based on their membership in the female or male half of the human race."[81] These are culturally shared beliefs about what men and women are like and how they should act, and they explain how we try to conform our own behaviors—and those of others—to these stereotypes in order to fit into adopted cultural norms and standards.

Undoubtedly, ideas about femininity and masculinity have had an enormous impact on culture and society at all levels, and there are several psychological and sociological theories as to how males and females acquire their gender identity. Some of these include evolutionary and sociobiological explanations, or theories based on more recent research involving the role of cognition and brain development in our capacity to comprehend sex-based dichotomies. Aspects of Freudian psychoanalytic theories of the role of sexuality in child rearing remain culturally relevant today—even when we might not be aware that we are invoking Victorian-era science!

Even our earliest and most revered philosophers offered theories about gender acquisition. And be it Plato or Aristotle, the notion of the inferiority of women was embraced and taught. These lauded Western civilization thinkers espoused the idea of women as incomplete, inferior, defective versions of the male species. The "woman as defective man" motif influenced our natural and social sciences, appearing in the writings of men from Thomas Aquinas to Sigmund Freud. Of course, their profound views were powerful in supporting the subjugation of women in all aspects of society and the law.

While there is no one universally accepted theory of gender identity acquisition, one of the most powerful theories is that of

---

81   Hilary M. Lips, *Sex & Gender: An Introduction*, 7th ed. (Long Grove, IL: Waveland Press, 2020).

Social Learning Theory/Social Cognitive Theory, led by psychologist Albert Bandura.[82] In a nutshell, his theory suggests that we develop both gender identity and gender roles through a learning process. According to this worldview, via processes of rewards, punishments, and reinforcements, we are socialized to become boys and girls, men and women. Gender socialization starts very early in our lives, and "role models" are extensive, including not only other human beings, but the media we watch, the toys we play with, and even the language we use. Gender socialization starts early, underscoring the most important three words in our lives. No, it's not "I love you." It's the pronouncement "It's a boy" or "It's a girl," typically just seconds following birth. Of course, with today's technology to know the sex of a baby while in utero, the pronouncement and subsequent conforming to established gender norms is starting ever and ever earlier in our lives.

Children learn behaviors that are gender-role appropriate and are rewarded or punished accordingly. As researchers learn more about the role of the brain and cognitive processes, Social Learning Theory has been modified over time, incorporating a view of the child as an active participant in the socialization process recognizing that cognitive abilities are important in this process.[83] In this modification of the theory, children learn at a very young age to discriminate between conduct that is appropriate for girls and conduct that is appropriate for boys and then begin to evaluate and regulate their own behavior based on this knowledge, quickly learning what behaviors are acceptable to exhibit (e.g., appropriate toys, clothing, and so on).

---

82   Albert Bandura, *Social Learning Theory* (Englewood Cliffs, N.J.: Prentice Hall, 1977).
83   Kay Bussey and Albert Bandura, "Social Cognitive Theory of Gender Development and Differentiation," *Psychological Review* 106, no. 4 (1999): 676-713, https://www.researchgate.net/publication/12741492_Social_Cognitive_Theory_of_Gender_Development_and_Differentiation.

Researchers have continued to build on these earlier models, further highlighting the role of society and culture. Clearly, the impact of gender roles and rules on a child's social world begins very early, and one big part of that impact is that boys learn to expect more choices and more power and more control over their lives than girls do.[84]

Gender socialization during a person's childhood significantly contributes to the perception of gender throughout his or her life. Our socialization, and the stereotypes this produces and that we learn to utilize about women and men, do not exist in a social vacuum. Throughout history, we have seen hierarchical relationships between men and women: men have held more social power than women; men have been dominant and women subordinate. As Lips points out, one function of stereotypes is to bolster the status quo. Hence, it is not surprising that dominant groups are ascribed values of greater competence and intelligence than are subordinate groups, and that groups with low social power are more likely to be stereotyped as emotional and incompetent.[85]

Our stereotypes are dynamic and depend on social context; hence, we can and have witnessed variability of our learned gender stereotypes not only across social or cultural groups, but across historical periods as well. Nonetheless, many of our perceptions of "femininity" and "masculinity" have remained quite persistent, and transgressing them may involve negative reactions from others.[86]

Hence, before we are even born, mechanisms exist to teach boys and girls a different set of expectations that help us understand how

---

84 Hilary M. Lips, *Sex & Gender: An Introduction,* 7th ed. (Long Grove, IL: Waveland Press, 2020), 416.

85 Hilary M. Lips, *Sex & Gender: An Introduction,* 7th ed. (Long Grove, IL: Waveland Press, 2020).

86 Hilary M. Lips, *Sex & Gender: An Introduction,* 7th ed. (Long Grove, IL: Waveland Press, 2020), 7.

"likable" we are. Overcoming gender bias necessitates that we examine how we become socialized into the gender roles we play and that others expect us to follow. So, let's take a peek at what we know about gender socialization and the very early footprints giving rise to these likability double standards we see in all facets of life, particularly the workplace.

LIONS AND TIGERS AND SLEEPING BEAUTIES, OH MY!

Gender socialization precedes even our birth as new moms and dads begin to prepare their lives for their anticipated new bundles of joy. Preparation of their homes often involves designing nurseries stereotypically adorned with pink or blue accessories, which have culturally come to signify girl or boy babies. Name selection, clothing, even birth invitations continue to suggest and reinforce persistent gender stereotypes, whereby birth announcements of a male baby typically convey a "tough tiger" contrasted with a "sweet beauty" if it's a girl.

When I lectured at the university, I enjoyed developing "field trips" to local toy and department stores to have students examine birth announcement cards and the array of clothing, accessories, and toys to reinforce the pronouncement of those three most important words made in our lives. The perception of the "It's a girl" or "It's a boy" pronouncement issued either in the months leading up to our birth, or seconds following delivery, become the most definitive methods our parents, relatives, friends, and others start using as a GPS system to shape who they expect us to become.

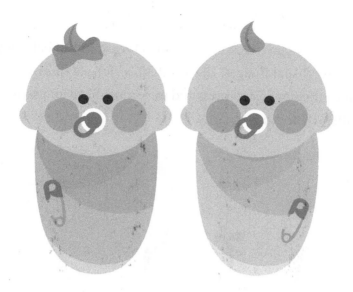

Parents are generally considered to be the primary source of children's gender learning, communicating different expectations for their daughters and sons from the first day of childbirth as documented by research interviews with new parents.[87] In this research, the new parents of daughters oohed and awed over their babies as more delicate than those with sons, while parents of sons gushed over their babies as being stronger, better coordinated, hardier, and more alert. These parental perceptions—particularly espoused by fathers—indicate gender stereotypes' influence, even though researchers found no difference in objective measures of the size and health of the infants. One study found that parents who saw an ultrasound picture and knew their fetus's sex described female fetuses as softer, littler, calmer, weaker, more delicate, and more beautiful than male fetuses.[88]

---

87   Jeffrey Z. Rubin, Frank J. Provenzano, and Zella Luria, "The Eye of the Beholder: Parents' Views on Sex of Newborns," *American Journal of Orthopsychiatry*, 44 (1974): 512-519. https://onlinelibrary.wiley.com/doi/abs/10.1111/j.1939-0025.1974.tb00905.x

88   J. Sweeney and M. R. Bradbard, "Mothers' and Fathers' Changing Perceptions of Their Male and Female Infants Over the Course of Pregnancy," *Journal of Genetic Psychology* 149, no. 3 (1988): 393-404, https://pubmed.ncbi.nlm.nih.gov/3062128/.

Social stereotypes reinforce these stereotypes. In a study of birth congratulatory patterns, cards intended for parents of baby boys had more active visual images. Cards intended for parents of baby girls contained themes of sweetness and were more likely to use adjectives like "little" than did boy cards.[89]

89   Judith S. Bridges, "Pink or Blue: Gender-Stereotypic Perceptions of Infants as Conveyed by Birth Congratulations Cards," *Psychology of Women Quarterly* 17, no. 2 (1993): 193-206, https://onlinelibrary.wiley.com/doi/abs/10.1111/j.1471-6402.1993.tb00444.x.

From infancy, parents reinforce gender bias in their parenting patterns, including a dad not allowing his son to play with Barbies and other dolls because these are feminine, or attributing boys' encouraged physicality and actions as "boys will be boys." Several studies reveal that parents treat their female and male offspring differently by giving them different toys, dressing them differently and assigning them different household tasks.[90] And when parents decorate, unsurprisingly, boys' rooms were more likely to display sports equipment, trucks and cars, or soldiers and weapons. Girls' rooms, on the other hand, were more likely to look pretty in pink, feature lace, and display dolls and dollhouses. Even with the passage of time, studies continue to show that the decor of young children's rooms was still markedly gendered by color (pink vs. blue), mirroring the color-coding in toy/theme selection.[91]

From infancy, we still tend to swaddle our babies in either pink or blue blankets, and this color selection carries into the clothing that we begin to choose for them. Once upon a time, men wore robes and kilts (umm, dresses and skirts) but it's not common to catch a male sporting this clothing in today's society. When there is gender-bending in clothing, it is more likely that females will skew male, as opposed to males donning clothing deemed female. Once upon a time, females were not allowed to wear pants or pantsuits to work, eventually taking new legislation to enact new laws to not punish women for wearing these clothing choices on the job. Yet, the pendulum has not swung the other way.

---

90   Hugh Lytton and David M. Romney, "Parents' Differential Socialization of Boys and Girls: A Meta-Analysis," *Psychological Bulletin* 109, no. 2 (1991): 267-296, https://psycnet.apa.org/record/1991-15054-001.

91   David MacPhee and Sarah Prendergast, "Room for Improvement: Girls' and Boys' Home Environments Are Still Gendered," *Sex Roles: A Journal of Research* 80 (2019): 332-346, dx.doi.org/10.1007/s11199-018-0936-2.

From pink tutus to Halloween costumes, societal stereotypes of what is appropriate for boys and girls are gendered. Girls are typically offered traditional feminine hero costumes: beauty queens, princesses, brides, and cheerleaders—"sexy nurses" as we grow older. Boys' costumes often have villain and warrior themes.[92] Have you ever wandered in the fantasy and adventure lands of Disney World or Disneyland? There is no shortage of little girls dressed as Sleeping Beauties, Snow Whites, Cinderellas, or even any of the princess "rebels" such as Ariel (who gave up her voice for a man) or Belle (who endured captivity as a pathway to love). I have yet to spot little boys clamoring for costumes of Prince Charming, or any of the other Disney princes, such as Eric. In fact, most of us can't identify any of the princes. Rather, we are more likely to see boys as superheroes, monsters, or pirates, including Superman or Spiderman—real action figures who don't waste their time on love and beauty. These findings alone perpetuate ideas like "monsters act angry and scary" but "fairies or maids are passive, nice, and submissive." All these factors contribute to personality traits associated with gender.

Parents are likely to assign gendered chores. A study of household tasks performed by boys and girls found that boys were more likely to do outside yard work necessitating some muscle strength (snow shoveling or mowing the lawn), whereas girls were more likely to do indoor chores (dishwashing, cooking, or babysitting).[93]

One of my favorite places to visit to assess the culture of gender in toy manufacturing was Toys "R" Us, before it permanently closed.

---

92   Adie Nelson, "The Pink Dragon is Female: Halloween Costumes and Gender Markers," *Psychology of Women Quarterly* 24, no. 2 (June 2000): 137-144, https://onlinelibrary.wiley.com/doi/abs/10.1111/j.1471-6402.2000.tb00194.x.

93   Lynne K. White and David B. Brinkerhoff, "The Sexual Division of Labor: Evidence from Childhood," *Social Forces* 60, no. 1 (September 1981): 170-181, https://academic.oup.com/sf/article-abstract/60/1/170/1938286.

One only had to walk in the front door to understand the significance of pink and blue and the existence of gender and perceived appropriate roles. The "pink" section was replete with dolls, cleaning and cooking utensils, and beauty costumes. A few aisles away was the "blue" section, replete with its trucks, action figures, and military warfare. I used to observe parents with their children as they went to shop for their desired toys (and developing gender identities) and would often hear the expressed angst of a little boy forced to walk down a pink aisle before allowing him to get to his section.

And make no doubt about it: an action figure is NOT a doll. Barbie is a doll; G.I. Joe is an action figure. What about Ken, you might ask? Ken will always be found in the "pink" section—arm candy for Barbie and instructive to little girls about what their Prince Charming should look and act like and that romance and relationships and attracting a partner is of paramount importance. Certainly, we've seen Barbie's roles progress since she was first introduced decades ago, and I once saw an astronaut Barbie—she even had her heels for walking on the moon. Geez. Interestingly, no baby dolls were ever stocked in the "blue" section of the store, a sad commentary on expectations for motherhood, fatherhood, and parenting.

Play and toys are important in the socialization of children, and we learn to dream who we are to become as adults. Increasingly, as time changes, girls have been encouraged to become doctors and firefighters and scientists. But when interviewed, girl children are still more likely to identify an outside-the-home career role but add in the role of "Mommy" too. Boys, not so much. Boys will talk of becoming those things as well, but leave off the "and a daddy too" as part of their adult identities and roles.

Toys foster nurturing or independence, reinforcing expectations about gender in the children we raise and who we are to become.

Hence, toy selection and preference are encouraged for boys and girls differently, and parents play with their children in quite different ways. Parents are more likely to talk with their daughters but to roughhouse and play actively with their sons. Parents are more likely to engage in performance and task-oriented play with sons, developing more general problem-solving strategies. With daughters, parents interact in more cooperative, sharing—*ladylike*—methods of play.

COMMUNICATIONS, TELEVISION, AND MEDIA MESSAGES

Gender stereotypes are a significant component of media messaging. Children in the U.S. now watch more than forty-four hours per week of TV, at surprisingly young ages. On average, eight- to twelve-year-olds in this country consume just under five hours' worth of entertainment screen media per day, and teens consume an average of just under seven-and-a-half hours' worth—not including time spent using screens for school or homework.[94] Coupled with listening to music, streaming movies and music videos, and reading, it becomes clear that for most children beyond infancy, media is the most potent and pervasive source of information about their social world. Learning to watch starts young, even in infancy.

TV viewing is related to gender-stereotypical attitudes among children and teenagers, and a plethora of studies show that the more TV children, teens, and adults watch, the more we subscribe to male-female stereotypes and traditional gender role beliefs.

---

94 "The Common Sense Census: Media Use by Tweens and Teens," Common Sense Media Foundation, 2015, https://www.commonsensemedia.org/sites/default/files/uploads/research/census_researchreport.pdf

According to the Common Sense Media foundation, children in the U.S. are spending hours each day watching not only television, but their smartphones, laptops, and computers as well. Additionally, Common Sense Media finds that the biggest change in young people's media habits over the past four years is the amount of time they spend watching online videos like those found on YouTube.[95] The percent of young people who say they watch online videos "every day" has more than doubled, going from 24 percent to 56 percent among eight-to-twelve-year-olds, and from 34 percent to 69 percent among thirteen-to-eighteen-year-olds. And the amount of time each age group spends watching online videos has gone from about a half hour a day to about an hour a day on average.

Not only are children and adults watching television and streaming video content, but they are also watching advertising intended to impact buying behavior. It is estimated that Americans view more than an hour of TV ads daily.[96] Gender is extremely influential in advertising, not only in its pervasiveness but also in its messaging content, which continues to depict that males are the authorities—typically being the "voiceover" in commercials to suggest voices of authority. Women continue to be under-represented as main characters in primetime commercials, except for those selling beauty products. Let me rephrase this: older women are either selling beauty products urging us to cling to our youth and "rewind the clock" or selling floor cleaning supplies and toilet scrubs.

Ads largely display women as objects to be looked *at* and judged by traditional beauty metrics involving weight and curvature.

---

95   "The Common Sense Census: Media Use by Kids Age Zero to Eight," Common Sense Media Foundation, 2017, http://cdn.cnn.com/cnn/2017/images/11/07/csm_zerotoeight_full.report.final.2017.pdf.

96   "The Average American is Exposed to More Than 1 Hour of TV Ads Every Day," Marketing Charts, posted May 13, 2014, https://www.marketingcharts.com/television-42660.

Though "beauty is in the eye of the beholder," cultural standards clearly impart messages of ideal femininity, leading to an observable correlational rise in women's expressed body dissatisfaction with their own body size. An anatomically and physiologically impossible doll—Barbie—has become the icon of beauty for most little girls (I remember my first)! The greater exposure to TV talk shows and "sexy" primetime shows among high school students was observed to be a predictor of how likely those individual students were to express agreement with sexual stereotypes, and watching more of these shows impacted students' endorsement of more gender and sexual stereotypes.[97] A more recent study found that TV exposure is linked to objectifying attitudes toward women.[98]

But it's not just watching television. Motion pictures, social media, internet chat pages, music videos, and even the music we listen to both depict and perpetuate stereotypical images of females and males. The sexualization of women is prominent in advertising. Findings consistently reveal that in TV commercials, women are shown in states of nudity and are more likely to be depicted as sexual objects than men.[99] Given the focus on beauty, it's hardly surprising that women are more likely to be displayed in implicitly sexual and subservient behaviors and the frequency of watching these commercials increases the probability that viewers will

---

[97] L. Monique Ward and Kimberly Friedman, "Using TV as a Guide: Associations Between Television Viewing and Adolescents' Sexual Attitudes and Behavior," *Journal of Research on Adolescence* 16, no. 1 (March 2006): 133–156, https://onlinelibrary.wiley.com/doi/full/10.1111/j.1532-7795.2006.00125.x.

[98] Ann Rousseau, Rachel F. Rodgers and Steven Eggermont, "A Short-Term Longitudinal Exploration of the Impact of TV Exposure on Objectifying Attitudes Toward Women in Early Adolescent Boys," *Sex Roles: A Journal of Research* 80 (2019): 186-199, http://dx.doi.org/10.1007/s11199-018-0925-5.

[99] L. Monique Ward, "Media and Sexualization: State of Empirical Research, 1995-2015," *Journal of Sex Research*, 53 no. 4-5 (2016): 560-577, https://www.tandfonline.com/doi/abs/10.1080/00224499.2016.1142496?journalCode=hjsr20.

judge women's and men's behavior in gender-stereotypical ways.[100] Such sexually objectifying attitudes toward women have been shown to be present in children and are associated with dieting and depression among girls and the endorsement of objectifying beliefs about women among boys.[101] Indeed, research shows that early adolescent boys express more negative attitudes toward gender-nonconforming behavior and experience greater pressure from peers to conform to and comply with stereotypical gender roles compared to girls.[102] Consequently, they are more likely to pursue and expect gender-congruent behaviors in themselves and their peers. [103] While Hollywood has made some advances in the representation of women in film, women still remain largely invisible, and increasingly disappear as we age. Even women cast as "action figures" still wear sexy little outfits. Is Wonder Woman wondrous because of what she does, or because what she wears and how she looks while she does it? Hmm...I wonder. Is the increase in female nudity and exposure of women's breasts in movies a sign of independence, or just another opportunity to own those breasts via gawks and stares?

Themes of misogyny and castigation of women as "bitches" and "hoes" are lyrics we've become accustomed to in rap music, partic-

100 Christine H. Hansen and Ranald D. Hansen, "How Rock Music Videos Can Change What is Seen When Boy Meets Girl: Priming Stereotypic Appraisal of Social Interactions," *Sex Roles: A Journal of Research* 19 (1988): 287-316, https://link.springer.com/article/10.1007/BF00289839.

101 Ann Rousseau, Rachel F. Rodgers and Steven Eggermont, "A Short-Term Longitudinal Exploration of the Impact of TV Exposure on Objectifying Attitudes Toward Women in Early Adolescent Boys," *Sex Roles: A Journal of Research* 80 (2019): 186-199, http://dx.doi.org/10.1007/s11199-018-0925-5"".

102 Henry M. W. Bos, Charles Picavet and Theo G. M. Sandfort, "Ethnicity, Gender Socialization, and Children's Attitudes Toward Gay Men and Lesbian Women," *Journal of Cross-Cultural Psychology* 43, no. 7 (October 2012): 1082-1094, https://journals.sagepub.com/doi/10.1177/0022022111420146.

103 Susan K. Egan and David G. Perry, "Gender Identity: A Multidimensional Analysis with Implications for Psychosocial Adjustment," *Developmental Psychology* 37, no. 4 (2001): 451-463, https://doi.org/10.1037/0012-1649.37.4.451.

ularly.[104] Women haven't fared well in most genres of musical lyrics, and young women who accept the sexual objectification of women in music videos are less likely than other women to be offended by potentially offensive sexual behaviors.[105] Lips, assessing implications of outcomes of this body of research on the sexual objectification of women in media, concludes that there are a broad range of negative outcomes: higher levels of body dissatisfaction, self-objectification, support for sexist beliefs, and tolerance of sexual violence against women. And, harkening back to our esteemed and exalted Plato and Aristotle, when subjects participated in experimental studies involving exposure to such media, it also resulted in reduced views of women's competence, morality, and humanity by both men and women.[106]

In the U.S., about 83 percent of girls and 97 percent of boys say they play video games on a computer, game console, or cellphone.[107] Only 8 percent of new games by developers feature a female protagonist. Games are still overwhelmingly oriented toward a hypermasculine stereotype—such as search-and-destroy missions, kicking and fighting contests, or male sports—and they frequently objectify women. The few that explicitly target females are either equally stereotypical—such as shopping games—or thematic Barbie

---

104 Terri M. Adams and Douglas. B. Fuller, "The Words Have Changed but the Ideology Remains the Same: Misogynistic Lyrics in Rap Music," *Journal of Black Studies* 36, no. 6 (July 2006): 938-957, https://journals.sagepub.com/doi/10.1177/0021934704274072.

105 Kathleen Boyce Rodgers and Stacey J. T. Hust, "Sexual Objectification in Music Videos and Acceptance of Potentially Offensive Sexual Behaviors," *Psychology of Popular Media Culture* 7, no. 4, (2018): 413-428, http://dx.doi.org/10.1037/ppm0000142.

106 L. Monique Ward, "Media and Sexualization: State of Empirical Research, 1995-2015," *Journal of Sex Research* 53, no. 4-5 (March 2016): 560-577, http://dx.doi.org/10.1080/00224499.2016.1142496.

107 Monica Anderson and Jingjing Jiang, "Teens, Social Media and Technology 2018," Pew Research Center, posted May 31, 2018, http://www.pewinternet.org/2018/05/31/teens-social-media-technology-2018.

options.[108] Female characters are not only underrepresented but often sexualized, more likely to be shown partially nude or wearing sexually revealing clothing, and with an unrealistically sexy body. Concludes Lips: "A few companies are marketing games meant to be gender inclusive or even feminist; however, for now, the world of video games remains largely a bastion of gender stereotypes."[109]

Similarly, books are full of gender stereotypes and stereotyped portrayals of females and males. Male characters outnumber females; far more stories are centered on boys than on girls, and males are portrayed as adventurous, brave, competent, and clever, whereas females are depicted as incompetent, fearful, domestic, and dependent on others to solve[110] their problems.[111]

We learn to think of masculine people as people in general (e.g., mankind). Language is what mediates our interactions with the world and is important for our consciousness. Finally, let me say: do *not* refer to females as girls in the workplace. We are adults, not children. Yet, male executives regularly refer to adult women as "girls" and that it is "no big deal" when I point out to them that it is against child labor relations laws to hire pre-pubescent females. I've never heard them simultaneously refer to the adult men as "boys."

From childhood leading up to adulthood, women are reminded to pay attention to the tone and pitch of their voice, as pointed out

---

108   Carolyn Petit and Anita Sarkeesian, "Gender Breakdown of Games Featured at E3 2018," Feminist Frequency, posted June 14, 2018, https://feministfrequency.com/2018/06/14/gender-break-down-of-games-featured-at-e3-2018/06/14/gender-breakdown-of-games-featured-at-e3-2018.

109   Hilary M. Lips, *Sex & Gender: An Introduction,* 7th ed. (Long Grove, IL: Waveland Press 2020), 426.

110   Amanda B. Diekman and Sarah K. Murnen, "Learning to Be Little Women and Little Men: The Inequitable Gender Equality of Nonsexist Children's Literature," *Sex Roles: A Journal of Research* 50 (March 2004): 373-385, https://link.springer.com/article/10.1023%2FB%3ASERS.0000018892.26527.ea.

111   Katarina Filipovic, "Gender Representation in Children's Books: Case of an Early Childhood Setting," *Journal of Research in Childhood Education* 32, no. 3 (2018): 310-325, https://www.tandfonline.com/doi/abs/10.1080/02568543.2018.1464086.

in a recent study relating to the perceived likability and competence of a woman speaker to the pitch of her voice.[112] Yet, if vocal cues are seen as indicative of likability and other gendered personality attributes, then one implication is to try to alter one's voice in order to achieve a more favorable impression. Indeed, voice coaches abound with advertisements to help clients develop their "leadership voice," and, in the process of such, to be taken seriously. But for women, learning to lower their voice in order to sound more like a man—and therefore more successful—can be a double-edged sword. In their search for competence in traditionally masculine domains, women are still challenged to be judged as sufficiently feminine. Unfortunately, movement toward the former portends itself to movement away from the latter—and a greater chance of being penalized for being "insufficiently feminine." This is just another example of women having to adapt to the expectations of other people because of gendered expectations. Coaching women executives to speak in a more masculine way in order to better match the "think leader-think male" stereotype or to fit into masculine workplace or political cultures consolidates gender stereotypes, rather than overcoming them, further exacerbating gender bias and penalization of women at both ends of the voice-pitch candle! Greater educational efforts to better understand the operation of gender bias stemming from voice pitch and facial appearances are needed to transform historically masculine workplace cultures—rather than demanding the individual women working within them to change themselves.[113]

---

112   Barbara Krahé and Lida Papakonstantinou, "Speaking like a Man: Women's Pitch as a Cue for Gender Stereotyping," *Sex Roles: A Journal of Research* 82, no. 1-2 (2019): 94–101, https://doi.org/10.1007/s11199-019-01041-z.
113   Emily E. Duehr and Joyce E. Bono, "Men, Women, and Managers: Are Stereotypes Finally Changing?" *Personnel Psychology* 59, no. 4 (2006): 815-846, https://doi.org/10.1111/j.1744-6570.2006.00055.x.

Finally, have you ever noticed how much of our workplace behavior is rooted in predominantly male audience sports talk? We use sports metaphors at work to describe and evaluate our goals and objectives. Consider the following:

- "Let's level the playing field."
- "He dropped the ball."
- "We've scheduled a kick-off meeting."
- "I'm not going to sit on the sidelines and watch you."
- "We've got to start the ball rolling."
- "It's time to punt."
- "Next we'll tackle."
- "Full-court press."
- "The ball's in their court."
- "Slam dunk."
- "Par for the course."
- "No holds barred."
- "Go to the mat."
- "Move the goalposts."
- "Monday-morning quarterback."
- "Swing for the fences."
- "Down for the count."
- "Knock it out of the park."
- "Touchdown/Score/Goal!!!!"

While I'm not necessarily advocating that we eradicate this language in our socialization, it is important to be aware of how language and communication is very much wrapped up in biases that have long been the "playing field" of one gender or the other. How we evaluate how women should speak is rooted in cultural and social biases that can and often do exist unknowingly, removing women to the end zones of a workplace (pun intended!).

It is important to speak out and interrupt if we notice remarks that demonstrate this kind of prejudice, such as "She is emotional" or "She is too talkative" or "She is not very caring," as these can affect how competence is perceived, and these are not labels that would normally be assigned to men in the same situation. They could have just as easily said women were articulating objections and concerns, but they chose the Neanderthal route, which is more common than what you might think! In my career, I have also realized that it's not just our language and tone that is sought to be controlled, but our very physical presence and being. I've actually been cautioned that I gesture with my hands, and that I don't sit down but actually sometimes stand while speaking. "That can be intimidating," I've been told. *Seriously?* I'm actually wondering if the new unwritten rules for how women should talk, speak, and move while leading dictate that women be tightly corseted so that we cannot breathe or move or take up any oxygen in a conference room! And women cannot always be the "gender police" in the workforce. Laws are written to be enforced, not only when women notice violations. I recall I was once asked if I called out male colleagues for describing women as "bitching and moaning" about a work plan senior male executives had hatched. In fact, I typically do object whenever I hear this language, only adding, of course, to the perception that I am strident, angry, and intolerant.

Some "female leadership coaches" encourage women leaders to become comfortable with sports-talk, and while this may dismantle some communication barriers, this is not a solution to our language usage. Typically, girls and women are still socialized to be responsible for making men comfortable with their presence. We shouldn't have to know a sports team and batting averages in order to be likable. Women have experiences that are unique to our gender: men will never be mistaken for a flight attendant or someone's assistant when they are really the boss.[114]

LEARNING READING, WRITING, 'RITHMETIC... AND DON'T FORGET GENDER BIAS

Outside of being influenced by parents as their foremost role models, children spend the bulk of their time with teachers as they begin to leave the home, starting in preschool. Schools, particularly for young students, are not just about reading, writing, and arithmetic. No, these are the first social interactions where children begin to learn social skills, make friends, and learn appropriate methods of interacting with one another. Classrooms set the foundation for expected behavior in a formal setting, as well as expectations other people begin to develop toward you, including teachers and fellow students. As such, educational settings are a very important context through which gender knowledge and practices are reproduced.

Teachers consciously and unconsciously play a significant role in gender bias by reinforcing gendered behaviors.[115] It is in these microcosms of society to which we send our little ones where they first begin to learn social expectations and appropriate responses

---

114 Janet Pucino, *Not in the Club. An Executive Woman's Journey Through the Biased World of Business* (Beverly Hills, CA: Deep Canyon Media, 2013), 44.

115 Heidi M. Gansen, "Push-Ups Versus Clean-Up: Preschool Teachers' Gendered Beliefs, Expectations for Behavior, and Disciplinary Practices," *Sex Roles: A Journal of Research* 80, no. 7-8 (2018): 393–408, https://link.springer.com/article/10.1007%2Fs11199-018-0944-2.

about gender and how to behave as a proper boy or girl through explicit and implicit rules transmitted from their teachers and peers. Through disciplinary interactions—both verbal and nonverbal—gender roles, norms, and expectations are transmitted from teacher to children. Indeed, children are taught to obey their teachers, and to aspire to become "teacher's pet"—to want to be loved by that new individual in charge of us when we are away from home. Teachers carry tremendous influence in shaping who we become as young boys and girls. And the socialization starts early. Preschool is an age group in which the salience of categories like gender increases its importance and understanding in very young children. For example, it is not unusual for teachers to line up children in rows of "boys" and "girls," or to greet them with "Good morning, boys and girls" on a daily basis.[116]

Rules are also enforced by disciplining boys and girls through "appropriate consequences" based on their gender, and research shows that teachers discipline boys and girls differently; for example, girls are more likely to recompense by cleaning, boys by doing push-ups. Studies continue to show that teachers are more likely to perpetuate behavior like allowing boys to speak without raising their hand or reminding girls, not boys, about their manners, such as saying "please" and "thank you."

Studies looking at gender bias in teachers' treatment of their male and female students have repeatedly found disturbing patterns. Whether conscious or not, teachers initiate more interactions with male rather than with female students[117] and pay more attention to

---

116   Rebecca S. Bigler and Lynn S. Liben, "Developmental Intergroup Theory: Explaining and Reducing Children's Social Stereotyping and Prejudice," *Current Directions in Psychological Science* 16, no. 3 (June 2007): 162-166, https://doi.org/10.1111/j.1467-8721.2007.00496.x.

117   Susanne M. Jones and Kathryn Dindia, "A Meta-Analytic Perspective on Sex Equity in the Classroom," *Review of Educational Research* 74, no. 4 (2004): 443-471, http://dx.doi.org/10.3102/00346543074004443.

male rather than to female students.[118] Teachers allow boys more than girls to talk and interrupt them—a pattern of women both being interrupted when they speak and allowing the interruption to go unchallenged, carrying into adulthood. Additionally, teachers' own stereotypical beliefs (such as girls being emotional, boys being tough) may impact their disciplinary classroom practices.[119] Overall, boys—and later men's—voices get heard. In the classroom, girls are more likely to be applauded for being quiet,[120] soon resulting in the observation that girls ask fewer questions.[121] Further, African American girls are more likely to be reprimanded for being unladylike.[122] The behaviors of African American girls are more likely to result in suspensions and other disciplinary actions,[123] as teachers try to conform them into adopting more acceptable, passive expressions of femininity.[124]

Indeed, children spend a good part of their day away from their parents and in the classrooms of teachers for several months out of the year. Yet, teachers are unaware that they are treating boys and

118 Robyn Beaman, Kevin Wheldall and Coral Kemp, "Differential Teacher Attention to Boys and Girls in the Classroom," *Educational Review* 58, no. 3 (2006): 339-366, http://dx.doi.org/10.1080/00131910600748406.

119 Feyza Erden and Charles H. Wolfgang, "An Exploration of the Differences in Prekindergarten, Kindergarten, and First Grade Teachers' Beliefs Related to Discipline When Dealing with Male and Female Students," *Early Child Development and Care* 174, no. 1 (January 2004): 3-11, https://www.tandfonline.com/doi/abs/10.1080/0300443032000103098.

120 David Sadker, Myra Sadker and Karen R. Zittleman, *Still Failing at Fairness: How Gender Bias Cheats Girls and Boys in School and What We Can Do About It* (New York: Simon & Schuster, 2009).

121 Judy C. Pearson and Richard West, "An Initial Investigation of the Effects of Gender on Student Questions in the Classroom: Developing a Descriptive Base," *Communication Education* 40, no. 1 (1991): 22-32.

122 Edward W. Morris, "'Ladies' or 'Loudies'?: Perceptions and Experiences of Black Girls in Classrooms," *Youth and Society* 38, no. 4 (2007): 490-515, https://journals.sagepub.com/doi/10.1177/0044118X06296778.

123 Kimberlé Crenshaw, Priscilla Ocen, and Jyoti Nanda, *Black Girls Matter: Pushed Out, Overpoliced and Underprotected* (New York: African American Policy Forum, Center for Intersectionality and Social Policy Studies, 2016), Kindle.

124 Jamilia J. Blake, Bettie Ray Butler, Chance W. Lewis, and Alicia Darensbourg, "Unmasking the Inequitable Discipline Experiences of Urban Black Girls: Implications for Urban Educational Stakeholders," *The Urban Review* 43, no. 1 (2011): 90-106, https://link.springer.com/article/10.1007%2Fs11256-009-0148-8.

girls differently.[125] Teachers tend to punish boys and girls for different kinds of behavior: boys for being unruly and girls for making academic mistakes. However, when praise is handed out to girls, it is more likely to be for good appearance or conduct, whereas for boys it is more likely to be for good academic performance or effort. What are we to learn from this? That girls learn that the route to appreciation is being "good," and boys learn that they are appreciated for their academic efforts. Boys are encouraged to keep trying when they make a mistake, whereas girls are told not to worry about a mistake, and the teacher spends less time encouraging her to keep working on a problem until it is solved, reinforcing beliefs that teachers just expect boys to be more intellectually agile.[126]

Gender biases manifested in classrooms daily impact how girls and boys feel about themselves, their talents, and their career aspirations. Not surprisingly, then, children learn to stereotype occupations by gender[127] and to indicate personal preferences for gender-traditional career paths and occupations.[128] Young women may also avoid careers tagged as "masculine" because of perceived future conflicts they may have to personally face if they choose these career trajectories.[129]

125   Els Consuegra, Nadine Engels, and Vicky Willegems, "Using Video-Stimulated Recall to Investigate Teacher Awareness of Explicit and Implicit Gendered Thoughts on Classroom Interactions," *Teachers and Teaching: Theory and Practice* 22, no. 6 (2016): 683-699, http://dx.doi.org/10.1080/13540602.2016.1158958.

126   Hilary M. Lips, *Sex & Gender: An Introduction*, 7th ed. (Long Grove, IL: Waveland Press, 2020), 445.

127   David Miller, Kyle M. Nolla, Alice H. Eagly, and David H. Uttal, "The Development of Children's Gender-Science Stereotypes: A Meta-Analysis of 5 Decades of U.S. Draw-a-Scientist Studies," *Child Development* 89, no. 6 (2018): 1943-1955, https://doi.org/10.1111/cdev.13039.

128   Nick Chambers, Elnaz T. Kashefpakdel, Jordan Rehill, and Christian Percy, *Drawing the Future: Exploring the Career Aspirations of Primary School Children From Around the World*, (London: Education and Employers Research, Quantum House, January 2018), https://www.educationandemployers.org/wp-content/uploads/2018/01/DrawingTheFuture.pdf.

129   Alexandra E. Savela and Karen M. O'Brien, "Predicting College Women's Career Plans: Instrumentality, Work, and Family," *Journal of Career Development* 43, no. 4 (2016): 335-348, https://doi.org/10.1177/0894845315602118.

Overall, we can see that "likability" is a learned construct, conditioned by years of social reinforcement and modeling as to the appropriateness of behavior considered to be feminine or masculine. It's not surprising, then, when we see the social science research literature showing us that while girls might have high self-esteem when they are younger, this begins to decline and becomes low by the time girls go into high school. It's not surprising when we see from the research that girls often learn to dislike other women as well as themselves when they see that women in our society are less respected than men. Indeed, gender inequities and biases affect so many children—and it only sharpens when they enter the workplace and see Heidi and Howard in action!

And one more thing: teachers in America are overwhelmingly female and do amazing jobs in, oftentimes, very difficult and challenging situations. I have been told by educational "suits" that educational settings (predominantly female staffing) are weak and, in the spirit of Jack Nicholson, can't handle the truth—or strong women leaders. I suspect that if any of those corporate suits dare walk into a professional development team meeting of its (mostly female) staff and utter that nonsense, they would probably get a deserving not-too-nice lesson in return (which, then, they'd probably go out and moan and groan that the women were bitching and moaning!). But my point is that all of us utilize unconscious biases as we do our work. This is why gender bias training is so important in our workplaces, but there is also a profound need to start this in our school systems so that, when we end up in a workplace, we are not compounding and perpetuating all the biases we picked up along the way.

CHAPTER FOUR

You *Want* to Be *Likable?* The *Double* Double Bind of the Angry Black Woman, Fiery Latina, Asian Tiger Mom, Menopausal Mood-Swinging Matriarch, and Other Bias Barriers

Once upon a time, a student in my Sex and Gender class told me that the greatest horror story of all time was Stephen King's Carrie. I pointed out that central to the novel is menstruation, menstrual blood, and women's hormones, and posed a question about what that might say about societal views of women. Then they really became horrified.

While women of *all* ages, races and backgrounds are negatively impacted by Heidi versus Howard gender biases held against them, women "of a certain age" or ethnicity are disproportionately affected. While White women, undoubtedly, experience bias, stereotyping, and prejudice against being an agentic female, these appear to wreak havoc on women of color. Not only do minority women experience the double bind, but minority women face a double jeopardy: they're female and a member of a racial and/or ethnic minority group.

Over the past four decades, Black women have consistently earned an increasing share of all college degrees conferred, and in numbers that surpass their representation in the general population. One would think that this pursuit of educational advancement and attainment would be manifested in increased representation in the private sector and in leadership roles. Yet, that is not so.

For Black women, the duo of gender and racial stereotypes has an effect that spreads far beyond the scope of likability. We know that Black women are paid some of the lowest wages of any group— approximately 38 percent less than White men and 21 percent less than White women.[130] Despite enrolling in college at notably higher rates than White men,[131] they will still make 35 percent less at the same upper-level jobs. Like Latinas, the pay gap between Black women and White men begins to form the moment they begin to work, but this gap is amplified by the sheer volume of Black women who carry their entire family's finances upon their backs.

---

130   Ariane Hegewisch and Adiam Tesfaselassie, *The Gender Wage Gap: 2018; Earnings Differences by Gender, Race, and Ethnicity*, Institute for Women's Policy Research (September 2019), https://iwpr.org/iwpr-issues/employment-and-earnings/the-gender-wage-gap-2018-earnings-differences-by-gender-race-and-ethnicity/.

131   National Center for Education Statistics, "Table 302.60: Percentage of 18- to 24-year-olds enrolled in college, by level of institution and sex and race/ethnicity of the student: 1970 through 2018," *Digest of Education Statistics* (2019), https://nces.ed.gov/programs/digest/d19/tables/dt19_302.60.asp?current=yes.

Here are a few more figures to illustrate just how damaging these biases can be:[132]

- Black women with bachelor's degrees and advanced degrees will make an average of 35 percent less than White men.

- For every one hundred men promoted to manager, only fifty-eight Black women are promoted.

- The average Black women loses out on almost a million dollars over her career compared to her White male counterpart.

Even in the same job, Black women get paid less across the board, but that doesn't hinder their ambition for leadership. Black women are just as likely as White men and more likely than White women to say they aspire to become a top executive.[133] Black women also ask for promotions and raises at about the same rates as White women and men, despite getting stuck below management level. More than half of Black women who want to become executives credit their desire to influence workplace culture, a motivation that no other racial or ethnic group of women was as likely to credit.[134]

LATINAS

- On average, Latinas in the U.S. are paid 45 percent less than White men and 30 percent less than White women.[135]

---

132 Jess Huang, Alexis Krivkovich, Irina Starikova, Lareina Yee, and Delia Zanoschi, "Women in the Workplace 2019," McKinsey & Company and LeanIn.Org (October 2019), https://www.mckinsey.com/~/media/McKinsey/Featured%20Insights/Gender%20Equality/Women%20in%20the%20Workplace%202019/Women-in-the-workplace-2019.pdf.

133 Jess Huang, Alexis Krivkovich, Irina Starikova, Lareina Yee, and Delia Zanoschi, "Women in the Workplace 2019," McKinsey & Company and LeanIn.Org (October 2019), unpublished data.

134 "Women in the Workplace 2018," McKinsey & Company and LeanIn.Org, 2018, https://womenintheworkplace.com/2018.

135 Ariane Hegewisch and Zohal Barsi, *The Gender Wage Gap: 2019; Earnings Differences by Gender, Race, and Ethnicity,* Institute for Women's Policy Research (March 2020), https://iwpr.org/iwpr-issues/employment-and-earnings/the-gender-wage-gap-2019-earnings-differences-by-race-and-ethnicity/.

- The gap is largest for Latinas with a bachelor's degree, who earn 37 percent less than White men, on average.[136]

- For every one hundred men promoted to manager, only seventy-one Latinas are promoted.[137]

The average Latina loses out on over a million dollars over the course of her career, compared to the incomes of White men, which also widens the wealth gap.[138]

- Latinas face a double-edged sword of sexism and racism in the workplace: as women, Latinas are stereotyped as less competent than men, and as Latinas are stereotyped as less intelligent than White people.[139] While many people assume that Latinas face a large pay gap because they're concentrated in lower-paying jobs, data shows that even in the same jobs as White men, they're paid less.

SO WHY THE PAUCITY OF WOMEN OF COLOR IN EXECUTIVE LEADERSHIP POSITIONS?

While most companies claim they are committed to gender equality, progress continues to be slow, particularly for women of color who face more obstacles and a rockier road to leadership.[140] As of this writing, there are zero Black women leading Fortune

136 "Weekly and hourly earnings data from the Current Population Survey," U.S. Bureau of Labor Statistics, (October 2020), https://data.bls.gov/PDQWeb/le.
137 "Women in the Workplace 2020," LeanIn.Org and McKinsey & Company (2020), https://womenintheworkplace.com/.
138 "The Lifetime Wage Gap, State by State," National Women's Law Center (March 2020), https://nwlc.org/resources/the-lifetime-wage-gap-state-by-state/.
139 In one study, Latinas were rated less competent and less worthy of hiring than any other racial or ethnic group of women, https://www.insidehighered.com/news/2019/06/07/new-study-finds-discrimination against-women-and-racial-minorities-hiring-sciences.
140 Mary J. Wardell, *Twice As Good: Leadership and Power for Women of Color*, (New York: Morgan James, 2020).

500 companies in America. Former Xerox CEO Ursula Burns is the only Black woman to ever chair a Fortune 500 company in the list's history. (In 2019, Mary Winston served as interim CEO of Bed Bath & Beyond for a few months before the company appointed a White male for the permanent position.) Several "explanations" have been proffered to qualify—and dismiss—the dismal record of Black women of color in corporate America, including arguments that Black women don't have sufficient representation in the workforce, are less qualified, or aren't interested in leadership roles.

Yeah, right. As economist Nina Banks points out, "Black women's labor market history reveals deep-seated race and gender discrimination."[141] Compared with other women in the United States, Black women have always had the highest levels of labor market participation regardless of age, marital status, or presence of children at home, but even getting there has presented barriers. In a study somewhat reminiscent of the Heidi/Howard study described in Chapter Two, a study was conducted with identical resumes, but these names were Emily and Lakisha, presumably an African American female. Results showed large racial differences not only in callback rates, but also significant differences in the quality of the resume needed in order to be called back. The Lakisha applicant got fewer calls and needed to have eight additional years of experience in contrast to Emily.[142]

---

141 Nina Banks, "Black Women's Labor Market History Reveals Deep-Seated Race and Gender Discrimination," Economic Policy Institute, accessed February 19, 2019, https://www.epi.org/blog/black-womens-labor-market-history-reveals-deep-seated-race-and-gender-discrimination.

142 Marianne Bertrand and Sendhil Mullainathan, "Are Emily and Greg More Employable than Lakisha and Jamal? A Field Experiment on Labor Market Discrimination" (NBER Working Paper, No. 9873, July 2003), https://www.nber.org/system/files/working_papers/w9873/w9873.pdf.

Not only are women of color more likely to be considered as token affirmative action beneficiaries,[143] but they are also judged as having less leadership potential and being less effective leaders than Whites.[144] Black women are and always have been well represented in the broader labor force, yet are typically not represented in executive leadership.

Lean In's "The State of Black Women in Corporate America"[145] report dispels the myth that Black women are somehow less ambitious. The 2020 report finds, "For every 100 men promoted to manager, only 58 Black women are promoted, despite the fact that Black women ask for promotions at the same rate as men." In fact, the report explains that Black women's ambition is in fact often discouraged. "Because we expect women to be kind and communal, women are often criticized as 'overly ambitious' or 'out for themselves' when they express a desire to lead," the report explains. "For Black women, this ambition penalty can be compounded in some contexts by stereotypes that unfairly portray Black women as aggressive and angry."

But as the report clearly concludes, there is overwhelming, persistent race and gender discrimination that severely disadvantages Black women and stunts their career trajectory. "Women are having a worse experience than men. Women of color are having a worse experience than white women. And Black women in particular are having the worst experience of all." It further explains, "Black women are much less likely to be promoted to manager—and their

---

143   Matt O'Brien, "Report: Asian-American Tech Workers Absent from Silicon Valley's Executive Suites," *San Jose Mercury News*, May 6, 2015, https://www.mercurynews.com/2015/05/05/report-asian-american-tech-workers-absent-from-silicon-valleys-executive-suites.

144   Ashleigh Shelby Rosette, Geoffrey J. Leonardelli, and Katherine W. Phillips, "The White Standard: Racial Bias in Leader Categorization" *Journal of Applied Psychology* 93 (2008): 758.

145   "The State of Black Women in Corporate America 2020," Leanin.org and McKinsey & Company, https://leanin.org/research/state-of-black-women-in-corporate-america.

representation dwindles from there." In fact, the numbers are stark and undeniable when comparing Black women and White men in senior leadership roles. The report finds Black women to be severely underrepresented in senior leadership positions, capturing a meager 1.6 percent and 1.4 percent of VP and C-suite positions, respectively, compared to 57 percent and 68 percent held by White men (even though Black women make up 7.4 percent of the U.S. population and White men 35 percent). Beyond the problem of lacking representation in leadership roles, the report cites an array of additional challenges that Black women face, including lack of support at work, less interaction with senior leaders, everyday discrimination (examples include the myth of the "angry Black woman," microaggressions, often being "the only," lack of ally support), and penalized ambition.

While underrepresented in the workplace, women of color are over-stereotyped due to their dual-minority identity. This bias is most commonly visible in women of Black or Latino descent; Black women are often stereotyped as being "angry" and "loud," while Latinas are stereotyped as being "sassy," "fiery," or "passionate" when they make their opinions heard. Despite these fiery, angry women enrolling in college at higher rates than ever before and showing more of a desire to advance than their White counterparts, women of color continue to be disliked and dismissed by their peers.

As we know, stereotypes can be described as standardized mental pictures that are held in common by members of a group and that represent an oversimplified opinion, prejudiced attitude, or uncritical judgment. Minority women in the workplace often find themselves having to overcome widely held stereotypes about themselves. Minority women in the workplace must not only navigate the labyrinth of career progression and bias impacting women as a group, but overcome the glass ceiling while experiencing microaggressions at the workplace and overcoming ethnic and racial stereotypes as well.

For example, Asian Americans are dubbed "model minorities," with many of the labels and stereotypes about this group being more positive in nature, although they are labeled as being passive or non-assertive. So, how are Asian women treated when they exhibit none of the "humility" expected of them? The "tiger mom" is the prevailing stereotype of Chinese parenting in America, in which tiger moms are perceived to be highly controlling, strict, and severe almost to the point of abuse.[146] As Ellen Pao, former CEO of Reddit, points out in her accounting of sex discrimination at her workplace, she was often caught between two competing and contradictory stereotypes of how Asian American women are supposed to behave.[147] During her trial, she was labeled with descriptions like "not the warmest person," "a bit too opinionated," "overly opinionated," "very aggressive," "too competitive," "a cancer." Her "tone" was disliked, as well as her "pushiness" and her sense of "entitled-ness." Yes, indeed: she was an icy tiger mom not befitting a servile Geisha-girl they seemingly desired, but only when that descriptor fit their needs.

She was depicted negatively in several press, online, and social media accounts emanating from anti-Pao harassers, unhappy that this "uppity" woman had dared to take on the company. Imagery of her as Chairman Mao was particularly popular. As I read Ellen's memoir, I recollected that I've been called those exact same adjectives. Interchangeable pejoratives for similarly talented women executives. One thing, though: I was never labeled Chairman Mao, although I would not doubt that there were Latin American strong-arm dictators to which I was compared.

---

146   Amy Chua, *Battle Hymn of the Tiger Mother*, (New York: Penguin Books, 2011).
147   Ellen Pao, *Reset: My Fight for Inclusion and Lasting Change*, (New York: Spiegel & Grau, 2017), 207.

In today's workplace, African Americans still contend with negative images that shape how they are viewed in the workplace and society at large. For Black women in the workplace, this glass ceiling may seem even more impenetrable. Black women are forced to confront the angry Black woman stereotype, which characterizes Black women as bad-tempered, hostile and overly aggressive.[148] From former First Lady Michelle Obama to Vice President Kamala Harris, African American women who are recognized as highly successful have been barraged with stereotypical depictions about their "anger" issues. Great sports legends like Serena Williams have been similarly depicted[149] In Williams's case, during the U.S. Open final, she received a code violation for coaching, a penalty point for breaking her racquet, a game penalty for calling the umpire a thief, and a subsequent fine of $17,000. But it was the way she was punished for her anger that sparked further outrage. Her reactions to the referee's calls prompted the Women's Tennis Association to denounce sexism on the court and in the game, asserting Williams's reactions to the referee's calls were no different from how many top players react in the heat of a championship game.[150] Yet, the umpire showed Williams a different level of tolerance over her outbursts than if she had been a man. "The WTA believes that there should be no difference in the standards of tolerance provided to the emotions expressed by men versus women," said the WTA's chief executive, Steve Simon, in a statement.

148 Jioni A. Lewis, Ruby Mendenhall, Stacy A. Harwood, and Margaret Browne Huntt, "Ain't I A Woman?: Perceived Gendered Racial Microaggressions Experienced by Black Women," *The Counseling Psychologist* 44, (2016): 758-780. https://journals.sagepub.com/doi/10.1177/0011000016641193.

149 Ritu Prasad, "Serena Williams and the trope of the 'angry black woman,'" BBC News, September 11, 2018, https://www.bbc.com/news/world-us-canada-45476500.

150 "US Open 2018: Serena Williams' claims of sexism backed by WTA," BBC Sport, September 10, 2018, https://www.bbc.com/sport/tennis/45468290.

Other examples of this stereotype being applied include First Lady Michelle Obama being called "an angry Black woman" in 2008 and Vice President Kamala Harris being derided as "a nasty woman." The *New Yorker* magazine ran a cartoon cover depicting the first lady as a machine gun-toting, afro-wearing Black woman, playing on images of radical terrorists.[151] Other Black women have encountered the stereotype, including television sportscaster Jemele Hill, who was slapped with that "stereotypical mainstay in the American imagination: the angry black woman." According to the *Guardian*, "When the stereotype of the angry black woman is evoked, it characterizes black women as irrationally angry, hyper-aggressive, verbally abusive, raucous and argumentative. When employed, the stereotype of the angry black women is used to discredit black women's standpoint, render them invisible in an effort to mute their individual and collective voices, and it dismissively couches their concerns as tantrums of emasculating emotions. This stereotype delegitimizes black women's justifiable anger in reaction to intersectional inequality based on their race, class and gender. Instead, it is a weapon used by character assassins, looking to shoot black women down…."[152]

According to diversity and inclusion expert Janice Gassam, the origin of the angry Black woman stereotype is believed to stem from the 1950's radio show *Amos 'n' Andy*, which portrayed Black women as sassy and domineering.[153] The angry Black woman stereotype has persisted, enabling double-minority Black women to become more

151 Suzanne Goldenberg, "US Election: 'Terrorist Fist Bump' Cartoon Misfires," *The Guardian,* July 14, 2008, https://www.theguardian.com/world/2008/jul/15/barackobama.usa.
152 Ameer Hasan Loggins, "ESPN's Jemele Hill is being reduced to an 'angry black woman,'" *The Guardian*, October 12, 2017, https://www.theguardian.com/commentisfree/2017/oct/12/espn-jemele-hill-angry-black-woman-suspension-nfl.
153 Janice Gassam Asare, "Overcoming the Angry Black Woman Stereotype," *Forbes.com*, May 31, 2019, https://www.forbes.com/sites/janicegassam/2019/05/31/overcoming-the-angry-black-woman-stereotype/?sh=6523b5141fce.

vulnerable to further marginalization, not to mention that persistent stereotype of Black women as hypersexual and aggressive.[154] The Jezebel image represents a Black woman who serves or seduces White male individuals and is sexually aggressive or deviant—and then there's Mammy, a strong but subservient figure.

Racial microaggressions are subtle and everyday slights and insults can include insensitive comments based on stereotypes.[155] The majority of qualitative findings suggest that people of color experience various types of racial microaggressions including being treated as a second-class citizen, being made to feel invisible, and experiencing assumptions about cultural ways of being and communication. Although theory and research on racial microaggressions have developed over the past several years, few studies have focused on the intersection of racial and gender microaggressions, or what is recognized as intersectionality. The theory of racial microaggressions has been expanded to include gender, sexual orientation, and other marginalized identities. The emerging research on gender microaggressions is focused on subtle expressions of sexism toward women, which can include both conscious and unconscious messages communicated to women.[156]

Research has begun to address barriers to Black women's leadership and controlling images that perpetuate oppressive discourses. Research shows that the burden of discriminatory practices in the

154 Patricia Hill Collins, "Learning from the Outsider Within: The Sociological Significance of Black Feminist Thought," *Social Problems* 33, no. 6, (1986): S14-S32, https://www.jstor.org/stable/800672?seq=1.

155 Chester M. Pierce, Jean V. Carew, Diane Pierce-Gonzalez, and Deborah Wills, "An Experiment in Racism: TV Commercials," *Education and Urban Society* 10, no. 1, (1977), https://journals.sagepub.com/doi/10.1177/001312457701000105; and Derald Wing Sue, Christina M. Capodilupo, Gina C. Torino, Jennifer M. Bucceri, Aisha M. B. Holder, Kevin L. Nadal, and Marta Esquilin, "Racial Microaggressions in Everyday Life: Implications for Clinical Practice," *American Psychologist* 62, (2007): 271-286, https://psycnet.apa.org/record/2007-07130-001.

156 Derald Wing Sue, *Microaggressions in Everyday Life: Race, Gender, and Sexual Orientation*, (Hoboken, NJ: Wiley, 2010).

workplace may result in African American workers who experience internal and external pressures to present themselves in ways that minimize visible traits connecting them to African American culture. This may include chemically relaxing one's hair to appear more Eurocentric, assimilating to coworkers' behaviors, whitewashing resumes, hiding minority beliefs, and managing and suppressing emotions related to racism in the workplace.[157]

Hence, Black women must learn to navigate a professional world in which they are heavily penalized by racism, sexism, and the intersection of the two and resistance or refusals—actual or perceived—to conform to particular stereotypes may result in Black women being further stereotyped as bitchy, cold, stuck-up, and humorless.[158]

All of these dual processes of actively not conforming to negative stereotypes about Black people while at the same trying to conform to organizational values can be emotionally, psychologically, and physically exhausting. Indeed, Black women have spoken about the emotional and psychological distress of having to deal with scrutiny and the fear of being "branded" if they behave in any way that might confirm the stereotypical beliefs of their coworkers.[159] Managing the degree to which one can be authentic at work is a salient and often challenging experience for African Americans in their employment.[160] These findings confirm and highlight the ongoing

---

157 Patricia Faison Hewlin and Anna-Maria Broomes. "Authenticity in the Workplace: An African American Perspective," in *Race, Work and Leadership*, edited by Laura Morgan Roberts, Anthony J. Mayo, and David A. Thomas (Boston: Harvard Business Review, 2019), 139.

158 Patricia Faison Hewlin and Anna-Maria Broomes. "Authenticity in the Workplace: An African American Perspective," in *Race, Work and Leadership*, edited by Laura Morgan Roberts, Anthony J. Mayo, and David A. Thomas (Boston: Harvard Business Review, 2019), 139.

159 Patricia Faison Hewlin and Anna-Maria Broomes. "Authenticity in the Workplace: An African American Perspective," in *Race, Work and Leadership*, edited by Laura Morgan Roberts, Anthony J. Mayo, and David A. Thomas (Boston: Harvard Business Review, 2019), 139.

160 Patricia Faison Hewlin and Anna-Maria Broomes. "Authenticity in the Workplace: An African American Perspective," in *Race, Work and Leadership*, edited by Laura Morgan Roberts, Anthony J. Mayo, and David A. Thomas (Boston: Harvard Business Review, 2019), 142.

sense of duality or "double consciousness" that African Americans have experienced in and outside the workplace for decades.[161] These controlling images have been central to the (unconscious) discursive justification of sexual harassment and violence, which Black women experience at higher rates than any other group, impacting their ability to become leaders and further advance.

Hollywood and the marketing industry have played deleterious roles in stereotyping women overall, but especially women of color, by using stereotypical identities to sell products. Specifically, the bodies of Latina women have been used and sexualized to sell products targeted to men, such as alcohol. According to Mary Gilly, a professor of business at the University of California, Irvine, Latina women in particular are eroticized in the marketing industry because of their frequent portrayal as tempestuous, promiscuous, or sexy.

These stereotypical identities have spurred from the idea that Latinas are hot-tempered, tempestuous, promiscuous, and sexy, including the "fiery Latina" and the "hot *señorita.*" Both stem from the fact that Latinas are continually sexualized and eroticized in popular programming and in the entertainment industry as a whole. Recent examples include Sofia Vergara's character on the popular television show *Modern Family,* but examples date back to the 1920s and 1930s, with famed Mexican actress Dolores del Río typically cast as the exotic and passionate lover and Carmen Miranda playing sexy and bombshell characters in the 1930s and 1940s. Quite frankly, I have never met a Latina dancing around the workplace with a basket of fruit on her head. Just saying.

161　Patricia Faison Hewlin and Anna-Maria Broomes. "Authenticity in the Workplace: An African American Perspective," in *Race, Work and Leadership,* edited by Laura Morgan Roberts, Anthony J. Mayo, and David A. Thomas (Boston: Harvard Business Review, 2019), 145-146.

But Latina women also suffer a double indignity from the stereotype machine. It seems that Hollywood can't quite make up its mind about how to portray Latinas, because Latinas are also more likely to be depicted as a sultry seductress or the "Madonna-whore," simultaneously stereotyped as the sexy bombshell and the virginal stereotype of subservient, silent, and chaste. Actress Gina Rodriguez's portrayal of Jane on the successful television series *Jane the Virgin* is one of the more recent examples of Latina women being portrayed as virginal or passive. While Rodriguez's character is almost the polar opposite of Vergara's, both perpetuate extreme stereotypes of Latinas.

Part of the problem and the reason why this stereotype persists is a lack of awareness that this stereotype exists, as well as a lack of understanding regarding the historical and cultural experiences of women of color. Taking time to learn more about the historic and personal lives of minority female coworkers at the workplace can be significant.

The last three decades have seen the rise of diversity officers and diversity initiatives in organizations striving for a more inclusive workplace, and while there has been diversity progress in the managerial ranks of organizations, the advancement of women of color has not dramatically changed.[162] As of this writing, there are currently no Black women Fortune 500 CEOs, and at the sixteen Fortune 500 companies that share detailed demographic data, senior executive and board positions are dominated by White men (approximately 85 percent, a number that has remained consistent for decades). And please, before you even say it, spare me the "But what about Oprah" example!

Oprah Winfrey is an exception. And as powerful as she is, she cannot be used as the token woman in power to justify the remaining dismal statistics showing the disturbing underrepresentation of African Americans—and all women of color—in leadership positions. This is especially important when we understand that the number of businesses majority-owned by Black women *grew* 67 percent between 2007 and 2012, more growth than women-owned businesses as a whole.[163]

Undoubtedly, being a Black professional in America has a unique set of challenges. Although Black professionals represent 12 percent of the U.S. workforce, they represent 8 percent of management occupations.[164] Further, Blacks continue to fill a minority of senior leadership positions across every major industry in the U.S.: only 2 percent of Fortune 500 senior executives are Black; likewise, only

---

162 *Race, Work and Leadership*, ed. Laura Morgan Roberts, Anthony J. Mayo, and David A. Thomas (Boston: Harvard Business Review Press, 2019), xiv.

163 *Race, Work and Leadership*, ed. Laura Morgan Roberts, Anthony J. Mayo, and David A. Thomas (Boston: Harvard Business Review Press, 2019), xi.

164 "Household data, annual averages: Employed persons by detailed occupation, sex, race, and Hispanic or Latino ethnicity," U.S. Bureau of Labor Statistics, (2017), https://www.bls.gov/cps/cpsaat11.pdf.

7 percent of senior higher education administrators and 8 percent of leadership and board members for nonprofit organizations are Black.[165] Additionally, research indicates that when women and ethnic minorities are appointed to executive or corporate roles, they may find themselves more likely perched on a glass cliff—in risky or precarious leadership positions that involve the management of organizations in crisis—than to find themselves in positions of stable leadership. In other words: a Titanic "leadership" position to navigate an already sinking ship. These positions can set up and further exacerbate women and minorities for failure.[166]

In addition to the discrimination that some still face, because Black employees are often a minority in their workplaces, they have different experiences and quite often different outcomes from their non-Black peers. Research has found differences in the Black professional experience in terms of hiring, performance ratings, promotions, and many other outcomes.

And despite progress, women of color are more likely to have their competence questioned and authority resented and resisted.

Minority status is positively related to creating facades of conformity as an initial step to understanding the experience of individuals who bring diverse values to the organization. Minorities feel pressure to create facades at higher levels than members of other racial groups. Pressures to conform to the dominant value system can be traced to the severe punishment of slaves for expressing themselves authentically.

Black women were found to experience many negative health outcomes, including anxiety, at a greater rate than their White coun-

---

165 "Leading With Intent: 2017 National Index of Nonprofit Board Practices" BoardSource, (2017), https://leadingwithintent.org/wp-content/uploads/2017/11/LWI-2017.pdf.
166 *Race, Work and Leadership,* ed. Laura Morgan Roberts, Anthony J. Mayo, and David A. Thomas. (Boston: Harvard Business Review Press, 2019), 16.

terparts. Repressing emotions like anger for fear of adhering to the angry Black woman stereotype may actually end up being more damaging in the long run. Witnessing Black women displaying different emotions, whether that be anger, sadness, or joy, helps to normalize it.

Diversity and inclusion training should focus on these unchecked beliefs and views that each employee holds about other groups. Employees should be given the opportunity to listen to the experiences and stories of women of color. Finally, because the responsibility of deconstructing racism and sexism is not just the burden of a woman of color, it's important to learn to speak up and speak out. When stereotyping goes unchecked, this gives employees the perception that this behavior is acceptable.

"WOMEN OF A CERTAIN AGE": THE WOCA EFFECT

Let's face it: Hollywood and most advertisers tell us we aren't supposed to grow old. If you don't believe this, just browse a few aisles at your local CVS or Rite Aid or Target or Nordstrom. Product after product is sold to prevent us from aging, developing crow's feet, sagging jowls, you name it.

On the other hand, aging is allowed for men and grey hair can signify a career of distinction.

In June 2019, five female anchors at NY1, a reputable local news station in New York, filed a lawsuit against the news organization, alleging systematic age and gender discrimination. The lawsuit was filed by Roma Torre, who was the first on-air talent hired by NY1 and one of the station's most recognizable faces. She was joined in the lawsuit by Jeanine Ramirez, Kristen Shaughnessy, Vivian Lee and

Amanda Farinacci. The five women collectively had more than one hundred years of experience at NY1. Ranging in age from forty to sixty-one, they charged that despite earning numerous awards, NY1 management had made recent programming decisions that strongly favored younger female and male talent at the expense of older, more experienced women. Furthermore, their male colleague, Pat Kiernan suffered no disparate treatment and maintained his on-air standing despite aging alongside them. It appears that men are allowed to age; women, not so much.

In filing the lawsuit, the plaintiffs hoped to not only "hold NY1 accountable" for allegations of "blatant ageist and sexist views," but also intended "to send a message across all media that this epidemic of discrimination toward older women must come to an end."

The lawsuit outlined several areas in which it said NY1 favored younger female and male talent, while simultaneously casting aside more experienced women. The plaintiffs reached a confidential settlement with the station in December 2020 that included giving up their jobs.

Even as state and federal laws prohibit age discrimination, a 2009 Supreme Court decision made it more challenging for plaintiffs to prevail, creating additional barriers to more senior women. A study by economists at the University of California, Irvine and Tulane University found "robust evidence of age discrimination in hiring against older women." The data show that it is harder for older women to find jobs than it is for older men. The researchers created 40,000 job applications for fictional job seekers and submitted them to a variety of online job postings. They made resumes for older applicants (ages sixty-four to sixty-six), middle-aged applicants (forty-nine to fifty-one), and younger applicants (twenty-nine to thirty-one). After monitoring responses to these dummy applications, results showed that the callback rate for middle-aged female sales applicants was lower than for younger female applicants. Nonetheless, callback rates for male applicants were not impacted by age.[167]

As the authors of that study observe, age discrimination laws may not deal effectively with the situation of older women who face both age and gender bias. Additionally, society places greater scrutiny on the physical appearance of women. An examination of one hundred top-grossing popular films found that older female characters were not only underrepresented, but portrayed more negatively than older males, including being unattractive, unfriendly, and unintelligent.[168] While we have not adequately researched these issues for women in the workforce overall, the strongest anecdotal stories and push for the inclusion of women in the workforce appears to come from—of all places—Hollywood, which has historically placed a premium on physical appearances. Increasingly, actresses like Catherine Zeta-Jones and Kim Cattrall have publicly decried the industry's lack of roles for women in their forties and older. Helen Mirren commented at a 2015 Hollywood awards luncheon, "We all watched James Bond as he got more and more geriatric, and his girlfriends got younger and younger. It's so annoying."

Aging in Hollywood is precarious.[169] Acclaimed actress Meryl Streep recalled how role offers suddenly changed the year she turned

167 Lauren Stiller Rikleen, "Older Women Are Being Forced Out of the Workforce," in *HBR Guide for Women at Work*, ed. Harvard Business Review (Boston: Harvard Business Review, 2019), 189-193.

168 Doris G. Bazzini, William D. McIntosh, Stephen M. Smith, Sabrina Cook, and Caleigh Harris, "The Aging Women in Popular Film: Underrepresented, Unattractive, Unfriendly, and Unintelligent," *Sex Roles* 36, (1997): 531-543, https://link.springer.com/article/10.1007/BF02766689.

169 Rasha Ali and Beatrice Verhoeven, "14 Actresses Absurdly Accused of Being Too Old or Too Fat, From Jennifer Lawrence to Olivia Wilde," *The Wrap*, October 5, 2020, https://www.thewrap.com/actresses-accused-too-old-fat-photos/.

forty.[170] "When I was 40, I was offered three witch [roles]. I was not offered any female adventurers or love interests or heroes or demons. I was offered witches because I was 'old' at 40." Maggie Gyllenhaal was turned down for a role because she was "too old" to play the love interest for a fifty-five-year-old man. She was thirty-seven at the time. Olivia Wilde auditioned for a role in 2012 but was rejected because she was considered too old at the age of twenty-eight. The actress who eventually won the role was twenty-two.

In the first global study to systematically analyze representations of older adults in entertainment media, "Frail, Frumpy and Forgotten: A Report on the Movie Roles of Women of Age,"[171] the analysis led by the Geena Davis Institute on Gender in the Media demonstrated that entertainment media reinforces ageism in society by erasing and stereotyping older adults, especially women. Female characters over the age of fifty are more likely to be depicted in stereotypical ways than male characters over age fifty, and gender gaps abound. Female characters over the age of fifty are four times more likely to be shown as senile than male characters over that age, and more likely to be shown as sickly, unattractive, feeble, lonely, homebound, or frumpy. No leading characters over fifty years old are female. Male characters ages fifty plus are more likely to be depicted as leaders than female characters in that same age span.

To add insult to injury, women have long been the butt of jokes and are stereotyped by our hormones. So, when a WOCA speaks up, she may be judged as being "hormonal," and when she *really* speaks

---

170   Jeff Nelson, "Meryl Streep Calls out Hollywood on its Youth-Obsessed Culture," *People*, December 10, 2014, https://people.com/movies/meryl-streep-calls-out-hollywood-on-youth-obsessed-culture/.

171   "Frail, Frumpy and Forgotten: A Report on the Movie Roles of Women of Age," Geena Davis Institute on Gender in Media, (2020), https://seejane.org/wp-content/uploads/frail-frumpy-and-forgotten-report.pdf.

up, she may be judged as having mood swings—and "frightening" the entire office. I was once informed that some of my colleagues "didn't know which Gloria would show up in the morning," invoking a stereotype of a woman hormonally out of control and the image of a menopausal mood-swinging matriarch.

It was always a cheap shot to blame something on a woman's period/time of the month—how insulting to now add menopause to that list. It just never ends for a woman, at any age: menstruation, premenstrual, menopause—it seems there is no stage of life in which a woman is not perceived to be beholden to, and at the mercy of, her hormones.

Both Hollywood and the advertising industry have taken these hormone stereotypes to the bank. The foundation of Steven King's runaway bestseller *Carrie* actually depicts a biologically naive teenage girl going through puberty and her first menstrual period, and the derision of schoolmates.

Stereotypes about "the curse" and "that time of the month," as menstruation is often dubbed, get carried across our lifetimes, becoming exacerbated as women age and enter menopause. This is particularly when "women of a certain age" are caricatured as the mood-swinging matriarchs, and a perceived "raising of a woman's voice in a workplace meeting" can get transposed into a claim that she's berating non-menstruating staff and suffering from mood swings. The answer? Drugs, of course. Medication or some type of therapy to "control" and tame their actions at home prior to surfacing in the workplace. One can peruse copies of magazines dedicated to older women to find advertisements claiming that spouses lost their fear of their menopausal wives once they were administered "the drug."

For too long, this nexus between age and gender discrimination has been whispered about, replete with anecdotes shared at the office's water cooler. Yet, it is striking how little research actually exists on the topic, even as the number of lawsuits pertaining to gender and age discrimination filed by working women is on the increase.

Today, one in three Americans is fifty or older, and by 2030, one in five will be sixty-five and above. As women continue to outlive men, they are more likely to have increased health care needs, are more likely to be widowed, and will have fewer years in the workforce to accumulate post-retirement savings and sufficient social security. Managers need to recognize and root out these biases against older women to ensure a workforce where all generations are embraced for the talents they bring and a workplace that provides equal opportunities for women of all ages.

CHAPTER FIVE

Know Their Names: From Executive Suites to Courthouse Chambers—Historic Gender Bias and Likability Challenges

Ann Hopkins in 1990, the year of her final court victory in her struggle against sex discrimination in the workplace. She had sued the accounting firm Price Waterhouse arguing that it had passed her over for partner because of her "macho" demeanor. She died at age seventy-four. Credit: George Tames/*The New York Times*

It was the Civil Rights Act of 1964 which made it unlawful for employers to "fail or refuse to hire or to discharge any individual, or otherwise to discriminate against any individual with respect to his compensation terms, conditions, or privileges of employment, because of such individual's race, color, religion, sex, or national origin."

Yet, the irony behind the enactment of that law has seldom been shared. Ironically, the original draft legislation did not include sex in its intent, only amended into the bill by a Virginia segregationist, Representative Howard Smith, who openly opposed any type of legislation to end racial discrimination—the original scope of the bill. In what he perceived to be a clever poison pill that would dismantle the entire effort, he introduced the one-word amendment—"sex"—into the bill prior to debate, a move that caused derision and laughter by fellow members of Congress. Yet, after a seventy-five-day filibuster launched by Senate Democrats, President Lyndon B. Johnson signed the bill on July 2, 1964, just two days before national Independence Day commemorations.

One word—thought of as a joke when introduced—has made all the difference in the fight for equality in this nation. And just as one word can change a nation, so too can the actions of one brave individual.

We pay tribute to Rosa Parks as the mother of the modern American civil rights movement. By refusing to move to the back of the bus and standing—er, sitting—her ground on that city bus, she changed the course of history, inspiring girls and women to understand their worth.

And we know the name of the Honorable Supreme Court Justice Ruth Bader Ginsburg who has become an icon to young people as "the notorious RBG." Her story has been captured in a blockbuster

Hollywood film, as well as in numerous books written about her fight for equality on the basis of sex and eventual appointment to the Supreme Court. In a biography about her life, the early blatant sexism faced by Ginsburg was rampant. "The men bestowed derogatory nicknames upon their female classmates. Ginsburg's were 'Ruthless Ruthie' and, she later learned, 'Bitch.' 'Better Bitch than Mouse,' she responded."[172] Her story is one of being told that she was not exactly likable, and that she needed to modify how she moved, spoke, and presented herself to a jury that was to hear one of the most important legal cases ever to be heard by the highest courts in the nation. A court that heard her deliver a timeless appeal for the ages, "I ask no favor for my sex. All I ask of our brethren is that they take their feet off our necks," quoting the nineteenth-century abolitionist and advocate for women's suffrage, Sarah Grimké.[173] She had spoken for ten minutes without a single interruption from the justices, stunning them into silence.[174]

Many of us have learned about Congressmember Eleanor Holmes Norton, who as a civil rights attorney represented women employed at *Newsweek* magazine in 1970. At the time, the magazine's editors didn't believe that female researchers, newspaper clippers, or mail *girls* were capable of being writers and blatantly stated, "Women don't write." These female employees were called "dollies" by their male bosses.[175] Then, forty-six female staffers announced they were suing for gender discrimination—the first such suit filed against a U.S. employer.

---

172   Jane Sherron De Hart, *Ruth Bader Ginsburg: A Life* (New York: Alfred A. Knopf, 2018): 38.
173   Jane Sherron De Hart, *Ruth Bader Ginsburg: A Life* (New York: Alfred A. Knopf, 2018): 207.
174   Irin Carmon and Shana Knizhnik, *Notorious RBG: The Life and Times of Ruth Bader Ginsburg* (New York: Harper Collins, 2015): 46.
175   Jessica Bennett, *Feminist Fight Club: An Office Survival Manual for a Sexist Workplace* (New York: Harper Collins, 2016): xxiii.

"In the '60s and '70s, only men were hired as writers," says Lucy Howard, who was then a *Newsweek* researcher. "It was the system, and we accepted it—until we didn't. The women's movement was growing and we awakened to the notion that something was very wrong. Slowly and surreptitiously we talked, organized, often quietly in the ladies' room or over lunch at a restaurant appropriately named the Womens' Exchange," Howard says. "We grew in numbers, found a lawyer—Eleanor Holmes Norton—and finally we filed."[176]

The case of Ellen Pao, an Asian-American woman who took on Silicon Valley, has garnered some media attention. Pao had been working for six years at the Silicon Valley firm Kleiner Perkins Caufield & Byers, now Kleiner Perkins, as a junior partner and chief of staff for managing partner John Doerr when she filed a sex discrimination suit. Although she did not prevail in her case, which went to trial, Pao, who was warned by others, including women, to not sue because her career would be harmed, asserts in her memoir that, "Before my suit was over, though, other women had begun to sue tech companies with public filings. One of my lawyers represented a Taiwanese woman who sued Facebook for discrimination; her suit alleged that she was given menial tasks like serving drinks to the men on the team. Another lawyer at the firm represented Whitney Wolfe, one of the co-founders at Tinder, who sued for sexual harassment. Both of those suits settled, but others, against Microsoft and Twitter, are ongoing. Some reporters even came up with a name for the phenomenon of women or minorities in tech suing or speaking up. They called it the 'Pao effect.'"[177]

---

176 Nancy Cooper, "The Archive: The Inside Story of How Newsweek Women Filed a Suit and Opened Doors For Everyone Who Came After," *Newsweek*, April 2, 2019, https://www.newsweek.com/women-file-suit-class-action-gender-discrimination-newsweek-history-1383618.

177 Ellen Pao, "This Is How Sexism Works in Silicon Valley. My Lawsuit Failed. Others Won't," *New York Magazine*, August 21, 2017, https://www.thecut.com/2017/08/ellen-pao-silicon-valley-sexism-reset-excerpt.html.

It takes courage to step forward, and until women are willing to take those steps—win or lose—we will be writing about likability and gender bias and sex discrimination for the next 400 years.

In this chapter, I want to introduce you to someone you most likely have never learned about, but the woman we should honor as the Rosa Parks of the "End Likability Double Standard Movement": Ann Hopkins. In the forward to her memoir, Mary Roth Walsh writes, "Ann Hopkins's case, with its revelations about how personnel decisions are often made, helps explain the durability of the 'glass ceiling.' In 1996, ten years after two Wall Street Journal writers coined the term....Employment discrimination has clearly followed women as they climbed the corporate ladder. Where once discrimination issues were largely fought at the hiring state, today's plaintiffs are more apt to be challenging promotion and partnership decisions."[178]

What is particularly disconcerting and should shock our consciousness is that this was written in *1996*, and yet, here we go—not again—but even still. Of significance is the further observation by Walsh that, "Over the years, a number of researchers have tried to explain the relatively small number of female leaders. In the process [both] behavioral scientists [and]....popular writers have picked up on these theories and have been quick to offer instant 'solutions'.... The message they send is clear. There is something wrong with women and if they want to get ahead, they need to fix themselves. But as we learn from this book Ann Hopkins did not conclude that she had to fix herself."[179]

---

178 Mary Roth Walsh, "Foreword," in *So Ordered: Making Partner the Hard Way,* by Ann Branigar Hopkins (Amherst: University of Massachusetts Press, 1996): xi.

179 Mary Roth Walsh, "Foreword," in *So Ordered: Making Partner the Hard Way,* by Ann Branigar Hopkins (Amherst: University of Massachusetts Press, 1996): xii.

Rather, Hopkins sued the bastards, charging gender discrimination. And for the first time, the U.S. Supreme Court was asked to examine carefully the role of gender stereotyping in employment discrimination. Because of her tenacity, her courage, and her willingness to not accept "the system" anymore, she paved the way in shattering gender bias and glass ceilings in America. She gave us not only precedent, but someone we can invoke in whatever way we choose to challenge the *just not likable* double bind in which we *still* find ourselves but are no longer just accepting.

Let's start with her victory.

May 1, 2019, marked the thirtieth anniversary of the U.S. Supreme Court landmark decision *Price Waterhouse v. Hopkins*. Her court victory is recognized as a major Supreme Court workplace-discrimination case stemming from her denial of promotion at a large accounting firm and whose case formed the basis of later gender-discrimination rulings. Amazingly, few even know about this case. Yet, Hopkins should be known as the mother of the movement to end gender bias in her historic quest to not only smash the glass ceiling, but through her courage and fortitude to hold her own workplace accountable.

Hopkins was a senior manager in an office of Price Waterhouse, a nationwide professional accounting firm, when she was proposed for partnership in 1982. At Price Waterhouse, a senior manager becomes a candidate for partnership when the partners in her local office submit her name as a candidate. All other firm partners are then invited to submit written comments on each candidate. After reviewing the comments and interviewing the partners who submitted reviews, the firm's admissions committee makes a recommendation to the policy board. This recommendation will be either that the firm accepts the candidate for partnership, puts the application on hold, or denies the promotion outright. The policy board then decides whether to submit the candidate's name to the entire partnership for a vote, to hold her candidacy, or to reject her. The recommendation of the admissions committee, and the decision of the policy board, are not controlled by fixed guidelines: a certain number of positive comments from partners will not guarantee a candidate's admission to the partnership, nor will a specific quantity of negative comments necessarily defeat the application. Price Waterhouse places no limit on the number of persons whom it will admit to the partnership in any given year.

Let's be clear: friends who knew her assert that Hopkins was the *first* person who would tell you that she could be "unlikable": abrasive, vulgar, relentless, and impatient. Yet, colleagues knew she was one of the strongest consultants that Price Waterhouse had in 1982 in its Washington branch, which had led branch managers to nominate her for a partnership in the first place. She had billed more hours than any of her counterparts—all of whom were men—and had helped secure a government contract that was then one of the largest deals in the accounting firm's history.

Hopkins had joined the Washington office of the old Price Waterhouse accounting firm in 1978 and was considered one of the company's top management consultants. She developed computer systems for clients and was responsible for winning the firm's most lucrative contract, a project with the State Department worth up to $44 million. Job evaluations praised her as "a terribly hard worker" and "one of the very best."

Of the 662 partners at the firm at that time, seven were women. Of the eighty-eight persons proposed for partnership that year, only one—Hopkins—was a woman. Forty-seven of these candidates were admitted to the partnership, twenty-one were rejected, and twenty—

including Hopkins—were held for reconsideration the following year. Thirteen of the thirty-two partners who had submitted comments on Hopkins supported her bid for partnership. Three partners recommended that her candidacy be placed on hold, eight stated that they did not have an informed opinion about her, and eight recommended that she be denied partnership. She was neither offered nor denied admission to the partnership; instead, her candidacy was held for reconsideration the following year. Once again, she was passed over because management regarded her as "somewhat masculine." To improve her chances of making partner, Hopkins was told to "walk more femininely, talk more femininely, dress more femininely, wear make-up, have her hair styled, and wear jewelry." Known for her salty language, she was even urged to enroll in a course in charm school.

Refusing to accept the outcome, she stepped into history by taking the courageous steps to file litigation at a time when there were no such challenges.

Overlooking the quality of her work, leaders at Price Waterhouse had chosen to stagnate her and her career based on criticism of her as insufficiently ladylike, calling her macho, difficult, pushy, overbearing, and aggressive.

Hopkins resigned from Price Waterhouse, becoming a budget planner with the World Bank. But in 1984, she walked into history when she filed a job-discrimination lawsuit, suing the firm on grounds that her employer believed she was insufficiently stereotypically feminine and asking for protections on the basis of sex under Title VII of the Civil Rights Act of 1964 and holding her firm liable for discrimination.

In 1985, Federal Judge Gerhard A. Gesell ruled in her favor on grounds of "discriminatory stereotyping of females," acknowledging that "comments influenced by sex stereotypes" were key factors in denying Hopkins the partnership. However, he did not grant Hopkins the $1.2 million in damages she sought, nor did he reinstate her in her job. Hence, having come this far, she chose to pursue her case until it was eventually taken up by the U.S. Supreme Court.

She found vindication after waging a seven-year battle against Price Waterhouse that resulted in a 6-3 historic victory in the Supreme Court.[180] Not only did the ruling expand workplace discrimination protections to include gender stereotyping, but it has become the basis to continue to advocate on new legal grounds today, including the fight over transgender rights.

Partners in Hopkins's office who had supported her candidacy showcased her success in winning a $25 million contract with the Department of State, labeling it "an outstanding performance" and one that Hopkins carried out "virtually at the partner level." Despite Price Waterhouse's attempt at trial to minimize her contribution to this project, the court rejected their dismissal of her success, stating "[n]one of the other partnership candidates at Price Waterhouse that year had a comparable record in terms of successfully securing major contracts for the partnership."

The partners in Hopkins's office praised her character as well as her accomplishments, describing her in their joint statement as "an outstanding professional" who had a "deft touch," a "strong character, independence and integrity." Clients appear to have agreed with these assessments. At trial, one official from the State Department described her as "extremely competent, intelligent," "strong and forthright, very productive, energetic and creative."

Virtually all of the partners' negative remarks about Hopkins—even those of partners supporting her—had to do with her "inter-

---

180 "Price Waterhouse, Petitioner v. Ann B. Hopkins," U.S. Supreme Court, May 1, 1989, https://www.law.cornell.edu/supremecourt/text/490/228.

personal skills." Both supporters and opponents of her candidacy indicated that she was sometimes overly aggressive, unduly harsh, difficult to work with, and impatient with staff. Court defendant's exhibits revealed that some of the partners reacted negatively to Hopkins's personality because she was a woman. Several partners criticized her use of profanity; in response, one partner suggested that those partners objected to her swearing only "because it's a lady using foul language." Another supporter explained that Hopkins had matured from a tough-talking, somewhat masculine hard-nosed manager to an authoritative, formidable, but much more appealing lady partner candidate.

In support of Hopkins, the American Psychological Association filed a supporting brief, citing more than one hundred studies on stereotyping by gender. The Hopkins case incorporated a significant body of psychological research studies and became critically impactful in final deliberations of the court—following the precedence established by *Brown v. Board of Education* which had similarly relied upon the studies of psychologists Drs. Mamie and Kenneth Clark to help the Supreme Court understand the pernicious impacts of segregation on Black children. Similarly, Dr. Susan Fiske, a social psychologist, testified at trial that the partnership selection process at Price Waterhouse was likely influenced by sex stereotyping. Her testimony focused not only on the overtly sex-based comments of partners but also on gender-neutral remarks, made by partners who knew Hopkins only slightly, that were intensely critical of her. One partner, for example, baldly stated that Hopkins was "universally disliked" by staff and another described her as "consistently annoying and irritating." Yet these were people who had had very little contact with Hopkins. According to Fiske, Hopkins's uniqueness (as the only woman in the pool of candidates) and the subjectivity of the evaluations made it likely that sharply critical remarks such as these were the product of sex stereotyping—although Fiske admitted that she could not say with certainty whether any particular comment was the result of stereotyping. Fiske based her opinion on a review of the submitted comments, explaining that it was commonly accepted practice for social psychologists to reach this kind of conclusion without having met any of the people involved in the decision-making process.

Ultimately, the U.S. Supreme Court, which heard her appeal when she sued under Title VII of the Civil Rights Act, agreed she had a case for discrimination. "Even if we knew that Hopkins had 'personality problems,' this would not tell us that the partners who cast their evaluations of Hopkins in sex-based terms would have criticized her as sharply (or criticized her at all) if she had been a man," the decision read. "We sit not to determine whether Ms. Hopkins is nice, but to decide whether the partners reacted negatively to her personality because she is a woman."

In 1989, the Supreme Court ruled 6-3 that an employer had to demonstrate that its hiring decisions were based on merit, not on discriminatory notions, including those related to gender.

"In forbidding employers to discriminate against individuals because of their sex, Congress intended to strike at the entire spectrum of disparate treatment of men and women resulting from sex stereotypes," Justice William J. Brennan Jr. wrote in his majority opinion. "An employer who objects to aggressiveness in women but whose positions require this trait places women in an intolerable and impermissible Catch-22: out of a job if they behave aggressively and out of a job if they don't. Title VII lifts women out of this bind."[181]

---

181 "Price Waterhouse, Petitioner v. Ann B. Hopkins," U.S. Supreme Court, May 1, 1989, https://www.law.cornell.edu/supremecourt/text/490/228.

The *Price Waterhouse v. Hopkins* decision was the first time the court ruled that gender stereotyping was a form of discrimination, clarifying that discrimination against an employee on the basis of the employee's nonconformity with gender stereotypes constitutes impermissible sex discrimination. The Supreme Court also put the burden on employers to prove that they did not discriminate illegally, once an employee had shown that bias played a role in personnel decisions.

In the last thirty years, dozens of lower court decisions have cemented this understanding of Title VII. In the landmark decision, the Supreme Court clarified that Title VII bars not just discrimination because of one's sex assigned at birth, but also prohibits discrimination based on gender stereotyping. In other words, it is impermissible to treat employees differently based on their sex and it is also impermissible to treat employees differently because they are not the right kind of man or woman or non-binary person according to the employer. The Supreme Court clarified that we are beyond the day when an employer could evaluate employees by assuming or insisting that they matched the stereotype associated with their group.

Over the years since, the ruling in *Price Waterhouse v. Hopkins* has also led to a substantial number of lower court rulings not only in favor of women, but in support of lesbian, gay, bisexual and transgender plaintiffs who argued that they too were discriminated against based on gender stereotyping. In fact, five federal appeals courts have explicitly ruled that transgender people are protected against discrimination under federal laws prohibiting sex discrimination, as have dozens of federal district courts and state courts.

Ultimately, Price Waterhouse was ordered to give Hopkins her partnership—seven years and several court rulings after it was first denied. She also received more than $370,000 in back pay. Hopkins rejoined Price Waterhouse, eventually retiring in 2002. Hopkins wrote about her career and her historic lawsuit in a 1996 memoir, *So Ordered: Making Partner the Hard Way*. The memoir is a riveting personal account not only of the litigation she filed, but of the personal costs she bore during the process, including listening to descriptions about her personality. She writes, "I felt as if my personality were being dissected like a diseased frog in the biology lab,"[182] and documents the trials and tribulations, the agony and the ecstasy experienced in her life during the seven years she was embroiled in litigation. Often a lonely battle, she writes, "I always needed a good friend, a stiff drink, or both to keep me company when I read the [Price Waterhouse] legal paperwork....The description of my interpersonal skill problems in the petition for certiorari was as vituperative as any I had ever read. I have seen child abusers more kindly described."[183]

Throughout her life, she never referred to herself as a civil rights hero, believing that what she did she did was a matter of principle. Hopkins died June 23, 2018, at her home in Washington at age seventy-four, attributed to acute sensory peripheral neuropathy.

With all due respect to Hopkins, I disagree that she was not a hero: she paved the way for women like me who have the courage to challenge sexist stereotypes about how women should look, sound, and behave. She is a name, a life, a battle, a victory I hope all women in America come to know, cherish, and pass on to future generations. May she rest in peace and may we begin to know her name and pay rightful tribute to this great American champion who did so much

---

182 Ann Branigar Hopkins, *So Ordered: Making Partner the Hard Way* (Amherst: University of Massachusetts Press, 1996), 197.

183 Ann Branigar Hopkins, *So Ordered: Making Partner the Hard Way* (Amherst: University of Massachusetts Press, 1996), 282.

to pave the way for strong women everywhere to be treated with equality under the law. Remember, all "bitch" means is that you stood up for yourself. Not only did she stand up for herself, but she stood up for all women after her.

Hopkins spent seven years in litigation. Her actions led the way to the most important gender-discrimination ruling in the nation, paving a road for the rest of us to follow.

CHAPTER SIX

Smashing Ceilings and Challenging the Likability Double Standard

One day when my daughter, Soledad, was in 6th grade, I picked her up after school. Once in the car, she immediately asked, "Mom, what does 'bitch' mean?" telling me that two girls had threatened her in the school's bathroom that afternoon, yelling *that word to her as she outmaneuvered their attempt to block her exit from the bathroom. I jerked the car over to the side of the road, and told her, "Sol, I want you to remember this day: all 'bitch' means is that you stood up for yourself."*

So where do we go from here?

In previous chapters, we have seen how the double bind of likability has had a deleterious effect on women, something for which women in the workforce pay the price, even if we never walk into that executive suite. Undoubtedly, we have witnessed tremendous transformations in gender roles over the past fifty years, but women remain underrepresented at the top, overrepresented at the bottom of workplaces globally, and are just not likable when we lead, according to research conducted across decades. Closing the gender leadership gap is vital in order for organizations to effectively perform.

Any number of books have been written advising women who lead on how to navigate the labyrinth, break the glass ceilings, succeed in the corner office, and fight executive sexism. Some extremely valuable lessons and recommendations are offered, and I encourage readers to review what they have to say.

But this book is not one of "those how to fix this in ten quick steps."

My favorite books while doing research for this book were, let's say, more bombastic in how they approached the theme. (Remember, that's what I was called once upon a time.) Books such as *How to Be Successful Without Hurting Men's Feelings* or *Feminist Fight Club*. These are satirical renditions of not just—to use that sexist language I've heard in the workplace—bitching and moaning about the likability penalty, but how to tackle it head-on.

Because if we don't, who will?

Today we easily put on a hashtag and send out #MeToo messages. But it took brave, tenacious women, like Rose McGowan, who had the *audacity* to fight back in real time. While others hid and partied on with Hollywood scumbags, she fought the fight and won it for *us*, for the women who will follow after. Undoubtedly, she was advised that this would ruin her career or cramp her social invitations, but she pursued the fight.

I'm not saying that all women need to suddenly decide to put their careers at risk. But imagine if one did. Or two. Or twenty. Or a hundred after reading this book and speaking out. If we stand together, it's harder to caricature and mow us down.

So, what needs to be done?

A problem as challenging and persistent as gender discrimination in unlikely to disappear without widespread transformation. This chapter does not purport to have a definitive "top ten" checklist of items in order to fight and win this battle. The overt history of sexism we have faced is strong, and it will take time. But there are immediate steps we can take—and should take—in order to begin speaking up, acting out, and looking out not only for ourselves, but for those who will come long after we are gone.

So, with this in mind, let's look at a few recommendations I have.

GET OVER A NEED TO BE LIKED!

As Margaret Thatcher—dubbed the Iron Lady as prime minister—boldly observed, "If you just set out to be liked, you would be prepared to compromise on anything at any time, and you would accomplish nothing."

In her book, *Dare: Straight Talk on Confidence, Courage, and Career for Women* in Charge, Becky Blalock simply declares that women need to get over a socialized need to be liked.[184] Let's face it: change is not always easy, and oftentimes it is those who have most reaped the benefit of status quo and the practice of gender bias that are the ones who should be the first to change—yet they don't (like those at Price Waterhouse who fought Ann Hopkins). In such cases, it is far easier and more assuring to one's personal egos to resist change and then become very unhappy with those who are "to blame" for bringing about change. Blalock writes about invaluable advice given to her by her father, who said, "You need to understand that if you are out front and driving change, you are going to have dogs chasing you. Change makes people upset. You can't take it personally or let it distract you. Dogs don't chase parked cars."[185]

So, if you're being barked at, you're probably doing something challenging status quo—keep at it!

For women, especially, ignoring the barking can be challenging because we are conditioned by our culture to *want to be liked*. Think about it: social media is governed by likes! Facebook, Twitter, you name it: we crave that unknown "friends" click those little links to tell them, what? That they *like* us? They don't even *know* us! Yet, like Pavlov's dogs, we have been conditioned to seek those likes, as though these somehow validate who we are. And this seeking is particularly socialized into girls and women, as we saw in Chapter Three.

Double standards with which we've been socialized dictate that if men display anger, it is appreciated, whereas women are expected

---

184   Betsy Blalock, *Dare: Straight Talk on Confidence, Courage, and Career for Women in Charge* (San Francisco, CA: Jossey-Bass, 2013).

185   Betsy Blalock, *Dare: Straight Talk on Confidence, Courage, and Career for Women in Charge* (San Francisco, CA: Jossey-Bass, 2013): 78.

to be gentle. Hence, women tend to be labeled as bossy and bitchy if they show aggression. Tina Fey comically outlines this in her book *Bossypants*, sharing this advice for us: "Don't waste your energy trying to educate or change opinions. Go over, under, through and opinions will change organically when you're the boss. Or they won't. Who cares? Do your thing, and don't care if they like it."[186]

And yet, as I write this, I'm looking at news reports out of Holly-wood and a tale of two actors: Tom Cruise and Ellen DeGeneres, both of whom have been accused of screaming and being mean to their staff. And in the case of Mr. Mission Impossible action figure Cruise, we even have a video of him ranting in a profanity-laced scream. Yet, news reports treat the two so differently. While DeGeneres is derided, shamed, and blamed for being a mean witch and bitch (and we have no video of her alleged "meanness"), Cruise is praised as heroically taking forceful steps to protect all. Quite frankly, that just nakedly reveals the double standard of who we "allow" to become angry and mean in the workplace.

---

186   Tina Fey, *Bossypants* (New York: Little, Brown and Company, 2011).

STOP VICTIM SHAMING

Stop writing books on top ten must-do lists to succeed or how to change supposed defects that women need to fix inside themselves to achieve success. To begin with, we need to stop writing books offering counsel to women on things they need to change about *ourselves* in order to fit in in the workplace and succeed! Those "Top Ten Things to Do in Order to Succeed" only give credence to a further blaming of the victim, reinforcing myths that *we* are the ones to blame and if only we can change our own supposed defects then we can succeed.[187]

I don't want to have a top ten list of ways women should change themselves. Sadly, many advice columns and women-oriented magazines too often readily point out all of the supposed defects that women need to fix within themselves, or how they are to behave differently, in order to enter the club. This book is not advocating such.

As one of the earliest treatises on "the likability question" pointed out, "most popular literature was full of warnings that women adapt to organizations as *they found them*. It was considered ruinous for women to draw attention to themselves—and thus to their presumed shortcomings—by trying to change how organizations were structured or run. We were told that we must adjust to the workplace rather than expect the workplace to adjust to us. In particular, we were urged to develop a greater appreciation for the workings of the hierarchy, and to downplay any reservations we might have about its effectiveness....Why should the entrance of women onto the public stage alter this?"[188]

---

187 Janet Pucino, *Not in the Club. An Executive Woman's Journey Through the Biased World of Business* (Beverly Hills, CA: Deep Canyon Media, 2013).

188 Sally Helgesen, *The Female Advantage: Women's Ways of Leadership* (New York: Doubleday, 1995): xii-xiv.

Some publications I reviewed as I wrote this book pushed this agenda, urging women to learn to play the politics of promotion by toning down our voices, restricting our leadership urges, and learning when it is advantageous to be warm, deferential, and avoid direct eye contact when leading.[189]

What are we, Stepford Wives? Hell no, no, and no.

As I did research for this book, I was so inspired by the courage of Ann Hopkins. She did not focus on changing herself; she went out and challenged the system. In her memoir, *So Ordered: Making Partner the Hard Way*, she shares a humorous story of receiving a poem written by lawyer Joe Scott. In part, it reads:

> "So to all who reach for things stellar,
> But are hampered by not being a feller
> There's hope in the end,
> If you choose not to bend,
> and instead, hire Kator, Scott & Heller"[190]

In other words, sue the bastards! Or file a complaint, or blog about it, or write a book. It's up to each woman who has been personally impacted by this pernicious, persistent double standard to do what is right for her at that moment, given her personal and financial considerations. But until we raise our collective voices, nothing will change. And change comes *from* us, not to be done *to* us.

---

189 For an example of such, see Bonnie Marcus, *The Politics of Promotion: How High-Achieving Women Get Ahead and Stay Ahead* (Hoboken, NJ: John Wiley & Sons, 2015).
190 Ann Branigar Hopkins, *So Ordered: Making Partner the Hard Way* (Amherst: University of Massachusetts Press, 1996): 362.

CHALLENGE THE "LIKABILITY PENALTY"

Sheryl Sandberg's Lean In organization identifies a number of ways that managers can support equality of women with men in the workforce, including directly addressing likability issues. Because success and likability are positively correlated for men and negatively correlated for women, bias has a ripple effect in how we assess, evaluate, and promote women. To challenge this double-bind penalty, it is important to learn the language of likability and to challenge it. For example, when a female executive is called bossy, pushy, or shrill, ask for concrete examples of work or behavioral performance to objectify the adjectives being used. Follow up with questions about whether male behaviors are similarly described. Document concrete behaviors.

A significant step toward accomplishing this is to begin to evaluate performance fairly. There are increasing calls to begin to do this as a result of a growing body of research clearly demonstrating that male performance is often overestimated compared to female performance. This bias is even more pronounced when review criteria are unclear, making individuals more likely to rely on gut feelings and personal inferences. Over time, even small deviations in performance evaluation have a significant impact on women's careers. A resolution to this may be gender-blind evaluations in hiring, and when evaluating performance, ensuring that managers are aware of their gender bias. Sandberg encourages specificity in what constitutes excellent performance and asks managers to explain the reasons for their evaluations.[191] When people are accountable for their decisions, they are motivated to think through them carefully. Others have argued

---

191   Sheryl Sandberg, *Lean In: Women, Work, and the Will to Lead* (New York: Alfred A. Knopf, 2013).

that the performance should be evaluated, not the individual. This is why it is important to have job outcomes and success metrics—did the individual meet them or not? Hold performance, not personality, as the measure of success.

Janet Pucino writes about the biased world of business and the circuitous journey women are expected to make in order to enter "the clubs" of historically male-dominated executive posts. She argues that "If performance is evaluated on how likable you are, then run for the door. You're doomed from the start if the key traits the company desires are described as 'collaborative,' 'relationship builder,' 'service-oriented,' or 'team player,' when no objective data or assessment system is in place to determine whether you hit those marks.... [Without such] you may end up with continually shifting priorities that don't jive with the overall strategy of the company."[192] As long as men and women still hold on to beliefs that men should command more,[193] women leaders are going to remain just not that likable!

This is critical for executive women because calls for pay for performance practices are gaining popularity, but the objective measurement systems have not kept pace with the concept. Without keeping pace, judgments will rely on heuristics and likability traits to determine performance and pay, factors which, as we've seen, have double standards for women.

Likability becomes key to club members, molding to conformity of the organization irrespective of performance and wins. Likability and relationships hold a greater value than diligence and performance. To some degree, collaboration is a double standard. Women are expected to collaborate with their colleagues while their male

---

192 Janet Pucino, *Not in the Club. An Executive Woman's Journey Through the Biased World of Business* (Beverly Hills, CA: Deep Canyon Media, 2013), 110.
193 Janet Pucino, *Not in the Club. An Executive Woman's Journey Through the Biased World of Business* (Beverly Hills, CA: Deep Canyon Media, 2013), 72.

peers are more likely to be exempt from such. Furthermore, in a Pucino-observed club-based culture, males are even more so sanctioned to withhold or not share information with others.[194]

And don't expect women to become your ally just because they are women. I have seen and heard about examples of male executives hiring former colleagues—primarily women—as subordinates, in a Freudian-type move to reaffirm that they are "in charge." The new hires feel a sense of loyalty and pressure to stand with him in cases of a dispute.

Until we see the facts, we can't act.

If you've ever joined Weight Watchers, what you'll see is that as soon as you arrive at the weekly meeting, you step on the scale for your weighing: no evading the facts. With facts in hand, then discussion can ensue. It's a great model for ensuring that we know the numbers.

PUBLISH THE DATA: MANAGEMENT AND BOARD DIVERSITY STATISTICS; DISCRIMINATION CLAIMS

Think about any number of adages that give impetus to outing the data: If a tree falls in the forest and no one sees it, does it really make a sound? Or the first step towards solving a problem is admitting it exists.

However you want to frame it, it is imperative to compile, write about, and speak out on the numbers we just referenced in the previous paragraphs.

I have spent a good deal of my career in education, both in the K-12 system as well as at the university level. Although about 76

---

194   Janet Pucino, *Not in the Club. An Executive Woman's Journey Through the Biased World of Business* (Beverly Hills, CA: Deep Canyon Media, 2013), 131.

percent of the nation's K-12 educators are women, when it comes to school superintendents, only 24 percent are women. So, in a field where three-fourths of the potential candidate pool is women, what's holding women back from the top job? According to a recent study by the American Association of School Administrators (AASA),[195] there are a host of issues, including unconscious bias on the part of those who make hiring decisions and the boards that oversee them. In an interview with *USA Today* following the release of their study, former New York superintendent Mary Jean Marsico said the experience of interviewing for superintendent positions can only be described as "eye-opening." Says Marsico, "It mirrors what happens when women are interviewed for leadership positions in business or when they stand for elections. We're seen as passionate but also at times as emotional. But emotionality for a man is seen as a strength. It's seen as decisive and strategic."

Another superintendent says that she was perceived as emotional, explaining, "There was a time when I had to make huge decisions on personnel matters and I was accused of making those decisions based on emotions, not facts. And I believe that had I been a man making that decision, it may have been perceived as, 'Wow, that's a strong leader.'"

Daniel A. Domenech, executive director of the AASA says it directly: "Both in education and in the business world, there's a boys club." In my career, I have heard school officials claim that education is a field made up of women who are "weak," so a strong female leader is a "mismatch." Because school board members are often appointed with little or no training, I have observed how they can

---

195 Swapna Venugopal Ramaswamy, "School Superintendents are Overwhelmingly Male. What's Holding Women Back From the Top Job?" *USA Today*, February 20, 2020, https://www.usatoday.com/story/news/education/2020/02/20/female-school-district-superintendents-westchester-rockland/4798754002/.

sometimes fall prey to maneuvers by male administrators curbing communication with female superintendents in order to project the female as a bossy witch inconsistent with a "weak" female staff. Research has actually identified the role of "gatekeepers" as barriers to women, and "how gatekeepers talk about women."[196]

Be it academia or business, to some extent, "Sexism has gone underground. Often you have a gut impression that an experience is gendered, but it's hard to know. We have to make the invisible visible."[197]

If you want to understand fraud and corruption, follow the money, remember? Well, if we want to make change, then we need to compile, report, and expose the data because, quite frankly, once one sees the data, the bias is glaring.

But just hiring more women into management positions will not eliminate stereotypes. While increasing the diversity at an organization is desirable and should be implemented, mere exposure to women leaders is insufficient. Organizations must take proactive steps to eradicate stereotypic biases.[198] If the glass ceiling is allowed to persist at the organization despite all we know, then the outcome will just be more women smashing into it.

Nonetheless, all companies should publish their diversity stats and litigation and claims against the company. And stop the silence of nondisclosure forced agreements! In these cases, state legislatures

---

196 Carolyn Bernal, Nadezhda Monosov, Amy Stencler, Ashley Lajoie, Alison Raigoza, and Nancy Akhavan, "Gender Bias Within the Superintendency: A Comparative Study," *Journal of School Administration Research and Development* 2, no. 1 (Summer 2017): 42-52, https://eric.ed.gov-/?id=EJ1158072; Susan E. Chase and Colleen S. Bell, "Ideology, Discourse and Gender: How Gatekeepers Talk About Women School Superintendents," *Social Problems* 37, no. 2 (1990): 163-177, https://psycnet.apa.org/record/1990-29463-001.

197 Phone call with Smith College President Kathleen McCartney, cited in Deborah L. Rhode, *Women and Leadership* (New York: Oxford University Press, 2017), 96.

198 "Women 'Take Care,' Men 'Take Charge' - Stereotyping of U.S Business Leaders Exposed," Catalyst, posted October 19, 2005, https://www.catalyst.org/research/women-take-care-men-take-charge-stereotyping-of-u-s-business-leaders-exposed/.

should take a hard look at considering under what circumstances these should be disallowed or curtailed significantly. Covering up allegations of gender bias and workplace discrimination should no longer be tolerated. Indeed, Ann Hopkins recognized these as nothing short of gag orders. This is particularly important in areas where taxpayer dollars are involved, such as funding by federal or state or local governments or vendor contracts with such. Additionally, and especially in public sector workplaces, the use of so-called "administrative leave" can be used as a punitive tool to dilute the power of women superintendents/chief executive officers by removing her from her day-to-day work. More analyses are needed as to how male "gatekeepers" to the boards that are supposed to oversee their schools may utilize these punitive measures as a means to discredit women leaders or engage in retaliatory practices against those who file discrimination claims.

MAKE IT PERSONAL: IT HAPPENS HERE, NOT IN SOME ABSTRACT UNIVERSE FAR, FAR AWAY

Yes, of course, every company should be required to train its current management team on recognizing the biased behaviors outlined in this book. It won't stop the behavior from occurring, perhaps, but the training will raise awareness of the behaviors that block women. This does not imply that women should be held to different performance standards than men. Awareness of his or her bias are significant first steps.

But let's not kid ourselves: perceptions are not reality, and when it's not experienced personally, the true magnitude of bias and the scope of its impact can easily be minimized. Male executives can go through the motions of sponsoring workshops and seminars, and initiatives and diversity councils, but these can be mere measures to "check the box that they are doing something about ending the glass ceiling, allowing them to focus on 'more important' or 'real' business issues."[199]

Survey results portend disturbing findings, leading to an article in *Fortune* with a headline blaring that "Men really are clueless about their female coworkers." In that 2016 PayScale survey, 67 percent of men reported that "men and women have equal opportunities" contrasted with only 38 percent of women respondents.[200] Author Nancy Parsons cites the results of yet another study in which male managers and professionals were asked about women being treated unfairly in the workplace. The response: "It's a problem, just not where I work." In that study, only 10 percent agreed that women are treated unfairly in their workplace.[201]

For any gender bias training to be effective, it has to be made personal. If it's not felt, not seen, not embraced, then it's not real.

In the first of a groundbreaking series of studies, Catalyst Foundation examined what they identified as the "obvious but unspoken—how gender-based stereotypes in business limit opportunities for women to advance in the workplace and achieve their potential,"[202] and urged all organizations to scrutinize the existence of

---

199 Nancy E. Parsons, *Women are Creating the Glass Ceiling and Have the Power to End It* (New York: Hybrid Global, 2019), 24.

200 Rick Wartzman, "Men Really Are Clueless About Their Female Coworkers," *Fortune*, March 10, 2016, www.fortune.com/2016/03/10/men-really-are-clueless-about-women-at-work-glass-ceiling-pay-gap.

201 Nancy E. Parsons, *Women are Creating the Glass Ceiling and Have the Power to End It* (New York: Hybrid Global, 2019), 4-25; Romy Newman and Christy Johnson, "What Men Really Think About Gender in the Workplace," *Fairygodboss*, March 10, 2019, https://fairygodboss.com/articles/what-men-really-think-about-gender-in-the-workplace.

202 "Women 'Take Care,' Men 'Take Charge' - Stereotyping of U.S Business Leaders Exposed," Catalyst, posted October 19, 2005, https://www.catalyst.org/research/women-take-care-men-take-charge-stereotyping-of-u-s-business-leaders-exposed/.

stereotypes to women leaders in their organization, particularly looking at these three criteria:[203]

1. **Would you recognize the subtle impact of stereotypes in your organization?** Because it is difficult to detect individual instances of stereotyping, it is important to use the right "big picture" metrics to assess the effects of stereotypes.

2. **Has your organization kept a pulse on how stereotypes affect women in your organization?** Catalyst research consistently shows that women leaders cite stereotypes as a top barrier to their advancement.

3. **What steps is your organization taking to combat gender stereotypes?** Diversity training may not be an adequate defense, especially since most training programs do not equip employees to recognize or avoid the subtle effects of stereotypes on their perceptions.

SCRUTINIZE AND SMASH THE CEILING, TEAR DOWN THE LABYRINTH WALLS, AND TAKE ON THE WHOLE ENCHILADA

Although there are multiple contributors to the perpetuation of gender inequality, research cited in this book provides evidence that gender discrimination plays a significant role in its perpetuation. Stereotypic beliefs about men and women are widely held and have proven to be resistant to change despite decades of social progress.

---

203 "Women 'Take Care,' Men 'Take Charge' - Stereotyping of U.S Business Leaders Exposed," Catalyst, posted October 19, 2005, https://www.catalyst.org/research/women-take-care-men-take-charge-stereotyping-of-u-s-business-leaders-exposed/.

In order for women to be successful in leadership positions, corporations and all workplaces must embrace gender diversity throughout their organizations from the top down and the bottom up and eliminate biases at the source. In workplace environments, many executives are completely unaware of their own biases. Companies and boards need to evaluate workplace cultures and how they operate as clubs, challenging not only the way executives and board members are selected, but their organizational performance appraisals and the roles these play in the disparate treatment of women leaders. Combating the "lack of fit" perceptions on which this disparity in progress is rooted is critical to any advancement.[204]

Some of these strategies need to include changing gender stereotypes, with the education and training to accomplish this starting in childhood and in our educational systems of learning. Demasculinizing existing organizational cultures will not take place overnight, but requires commitment and accountability by those in charge.

And once board members are seated, have they developed a policy or shared a mission statement specifically about gender bias? Have they implemented a policy on training to minimize and remove gender bias from the workforce they oversee? As Janet Pucino highlights, "It takes a great deal more to get men comfortable working with and for women"[205] and, still, women carry the responsibility (or burden) of making men comfortable with their presence.[206]

And stop the practice of enabling male executives to develop their own personal workplace harems! As pointed out by Pucino, women

---

204 Madeline E. Heilman and Suzette Caleo, "Combatting Gender Discrimination: A Lack of Fit Framework," *Group Processes & Intergroup Relations*, 21, no 5 (2018): 725-744.

205 Janet Pucino, *Not in the Club. An Executive Woman's Journey Through the Biased World of Business* (Beverly Hills, CA: Deep Canyon Media, 2013), 38.

206 Janet Pucino, *Not in the Club. An Executive Woman's Journey Through the Biased World of Business* (Beverly Hills, CA: Deep Canyon Media, 2013), 71.

often get locked out of "the club" right from the start when organizations permit new executives to fill key leadership roles with employees from previous organizations. Such personnel practices enhance already established long-term relationships and loyalties with these employees, which are subsequently relied upon when needed.[207]

Additionally, such in-group loyalty can result in positions being filled on characteristics such as gender, race, and religion that contribute to diversity stagnation. Without clear standards fairly applied to all candidates, hiring and promotion decision makers can simply rely on their own unconscious biases, stereotypes, and personal preferences. When several female employees of Walmart filed suit against the giant retailer in U.S. federal court in 2001 alleging sex discrimination, plaintiffs called attention to precisely these lax human resources practices. After extensive discovery and oral argument, in 2003 the plaintiffs filed an amended complaint requesting certification as a class action on behalf of current and former female Walmart employees maintaining that the discrimination faced by the original plaintiffs was systematic in nature and affected all women employed by Walmart. The lawsuit represented approximately 1.5 million current and former female Walmart employees, making it the largest workplace bias case in US history at that time. Ultimately, the Supreme Court did not make a decision on the merit of the claims, but rather it ruled the lawsuit was too large to constitute a class action lawsuit, prompting the plaintiffs from that case to file individual, regional lawsuits against Walmart. Sex discrimination lawsuits have continued into 2020 with greater success for plaintiffs.

---

207   Janet Pucino, *Not in the Club. An Executive Woman's Journey Through the Biased World of Business* (Beverly Hills, CA: Deep Canyon Media, 2013), 21.

The door becomes "wide open to discrimination if managers have free rein to follow whatever hiring and promotion principles that they think are appropriate."[208] What exacerbates and compounds this is people's lack of awareness of the influence of stereotypes on their judgments.

So rather than just opening the door and inviting friends in one's personal networking circle to move to the front of the line, blind applications are not only more inclusive and fair, but women are 25 to 46 percent more likely to be hired with blind applications or auditions.

FACE AND EMBRACE OUR WOCA

Over fifty years since passage of the Civil Rights Act of 1964 prohibited employment discrimination on the basis of race, inclusion of women of color continues to be "glacial" at best.[209] Women of color continue to face struggles to be hired, retained, promoted, and included at work. We are far from the notion that we live in a post-racial society.

Women of color continue to face not only glass ceilings, but also sticky floors and labyrinthine career paths. Both race and gender come under scrutiny, not only for objective work performance, but also for dress, hairstyle, speech, accent, and so much more.

Do diversity initiatives actually help? Well, I'm not arguing for these to end, but after decades of knocking on the door, and even gaining entrance and mobility over the past few decades, women of color remain dramatically underrepresented at senior levels.

---

208 Alice H. Eagly and Linda L. Carli, *Through the Labyrinth: The Truth About How Women Become Leaders* (Boston: Harvard Business School Press, 2007), 155.

209 *Race, Work and Leadership*, eds. Laura Morgan Roberts, Anthony J. Mayo, and David A. Thomas (Boston: Harvard Business Review Press, 2019).

Workplaces need to move beyond "managing diversity" and, by extension, managing skin color, looks and voice in the workplace. Rather than trying to "fix" individuals historically impacted and harmed by sexism or racism, "an intersectional (vs. individual) perspective is necessary to identify recommendations for cultivating inclusion that are rooted in social justice."[210]

And these initiatives must specifically highlight and address not just barriers imposed by race and/or ethnicity, but the prevalence and practice of gender biases as well. As pointed out by diversity expert Mary Wardell, "Women of color have always and will continue to be disrupters of the status quo through their leadership at work and in society."[211] She further asserts that the absence of diversity among board members ensures there is no credibility to hold the management accountable for anything related to diversity and inclusion. Rhetoric about their commitment rings hollow. Hence, she asserts, "the occasional woman of color C-suite level executive who is hired and who represents the diversity and inclusion statement and espoused values can find herself as a corporate unicorn, operating under an extreme Twice as Good pressure cooker."[212]

And just as women should no longer be forced to become the gender police calling out all microaggressions at the workplace, similarly women of color cannot be called upon to become the race and gender cop either. It takes a village, remember? And sisters in the house, who have paid our dues to be there, need others to vigilantly patrol alongside us, as well.

---

210 Courtney L. McCluney and Veronica Caridad Rabelo, "Managing Diversity, Managing Blackness? An Intersectional Critique of Diversity Management Practices," in *Race, Work & Leadership. New Perspectives on the Black Experience*, eds. Laura Morgan Roberts, Anthony J. Mayo, and David A. Thomas (Boston: Harvard Business Review Press, 2019), 373-387.

211 Mary J. Wardell, *Twice as Good: Leadership and Power for Women of Color* (New York: Morgan James, 2020), xxvii.

212 Mary J. Wardell, *Twice as Good: Leadership and Power for Women of Color* (New York: Morgan James, 2020), 32.

ACT UP!

Finally, it has to end somewhere. But first it has to start.

And that typically means that someone needs to raise her hand, raise her voice, just outright object to what is taking place, has been taking place, and will continue to take place if we just carry on the status quo over these next 400 years.

Remember the admonition that well-behaved women rarely make history? Color outside the institutional lines. Speak up, stand up. Make things *happen*, not just *happen to you*.

Silence, in this day and age when others have used courage to march forward to make things better for us, is just negligence.

Do you think it was easy for Ann Hopkins to challenge the system? Yet she did, and spent years fighting what consumed her life, but paved the way for so many of us. Yet, that glass ceiling still stands strong with those pervasive "bitch" stereotypes providing support structures holding it up.

I ran for the California State Legislature to make a difference. During my years there I saw strong women, aspiring to ensure that constitutional rights were made accessible and equal for all. I am proud of the strength of the women with whom I served, and on several occasions had to engage with strong men who sometimes supported us and sometimes opposed us. And even after leaving the legislature, I have continued to speak up, act out, advocate and fight for equal rights for women and to continue smashing that glass ceiling for all of us.

I reject the "leadership" advice I saw so much of, urging women leaders that "Until our culture evolves, as a woman, you'll have to do this within the context of the double bind. You'll often have to do better work than male counterparts to stay ahead, but you'll be shamed or gaslighted if you toot your own horn too explicitly. Find the forms of self-promotion that work—for a woman—within your workplaces. These will likely be subtler than those that typically work for men."[213]

Sign me up for the feminist fight club! We shouldn't have to hide, change, be silent, or shut up in order to be able to bring home the bacon and fry it up in our pans.

Women must rekindle our activism. Of all the Hollywood celebrities, I have the greatest respect for Rose McGowan, who had the courage and tenacity to take on sexual harassment and challenge the system long before hashtags made it fashionable to do so—and long before the perps started walking.

I get it: change can be frightening, especially when that yellow brick road to happiness hasn't exactly been paved and is marked by potholes and quicksand along the way. But if not you, then who? How do we *make* change if we ourselves are not willing to *be* the change? Ellen Pao offers advice for hitting reset, including creating what she creatively calls an "F-you fund" as an option to leave a bad workplace—or sue it! [214]

Undoubtedly, women who are considering making a formal complaint need to understand the financial, psychological, and reputational cost of pursuing it. In doing research for this book, I spoke with several female executives who told me they had been subjected to similar behavior but hadn't filed suit. Attorneys working on gender bias or sexual harassment cases typically work on a contingent fee, which means that their compensation comes only if they win a judgment. Finding a lawyer can be hard, as employment

---

213 Whitney Johnson and Tara Mohr, "Disrupt Yourself - And the Way You Work," in *HBR Guide For Women at Work,* ed. Harvard Business Review (Boston: Harvard Business Review Press, 2019), 24.

214 Ellen Pao, *Reset: My Fight for Inclusion and Lasting Change,* (New York: Spiegel & Grau, 2017), 265.

discrimination cases have the lowest win rate for plaintiffs of any civil cause of action.[215] And in gender bias cases, such as sexual harassment, it is the complainant as much as the harasser who is on trial.

Women experiencing the likability penalty and gender bias should make a record and document their efforts. Tell trusted friends and colleagues so that these individuals can serve as witnesses in a subsequent investigation or legal proceeding. Even if you think the incident will do nothing, you should still report it in a timely fashion. It is imperative to establish the record, to write it down, to share it with others. The more we openly tell our story, the more comfortable we will become in changing the workplace discourse.

Some women may decide to blog about injustice and make a change, as did whistleblower Susan Fowler over what she saw at Uber.[216] Others like Ellen Pao took on high-tech sexism, and while she did not win over a "jury of her peers," she won over the hearts and minds of women everywhere who understand that hers was a good fight, and her fight has made it possible for others to have courage, as well.[217]

In my career, I have filed a claim with the Department of Fair Employment and Housing. There are a variety of legal options and pathways available to combat gender bias, and each person has to choose what is the pathway that is best for her and will bring a measure of justice going forward. Going to trial can be quite expensive—does one have the financial resources and the time to potentially be tied up in litigation for years? What might be the

215 Joanna L. Grossman and Deborah L. Rhode "What to Do if You've Been Sexually Harassed," in *HBR Guide For Women at Work,* ed. Harvard Business Review (Boston: Harvard Business Review Press, 2019), 181-188.

216 Susan Fowler, *Whistleblower: My Journey to Silicon Valley and Fight for Justice at Uber* (New York: Viking, 2017).

217 Ellen Pao, *Reset: My Fight for Inclusion and Lasting Change,* (New York: Spiegel & Grau, 2017).

personal and family tolls? Not going to full trial is a viable route, but gender bias discrimination settlements often come with mandatory nondisclosures, which obscure transparency and compound the issue of bringing forth the truth publicly. At many workplaces, new employees readily sign mandatory arbitration agreements stuffed into a thick packet of paperwork to be completed as a condition of employment. Not really understanding the significance of these legal documents, and surely not anticipating that they will ever need these in the future, new employees readily sign. And then it hits, and one is forced to go the pathway of arbitration and mandatory nondisclosures.

To be honest, I knew very little about mandatory arbitration and the gagging nondisclosure agreements that typically accompany them until recently. These are critically important issues that state legislatures should address, particularly for any business receiving taxpayer dollars or doing business with governmental entities in any form. The #MeToo movement made strong headway with sexual harassment, but as we have seen, gender bias discriminatory behaviors can be a precursor to such and should be similarly prevented from occurring and throttled when they do.

As I write, a new bill by California Senator Connie Leyva has been introduced that seeks to build on a bold legislative agenda targeting nondisclosures that keep workers from speaking out about harassment and discrimination when leaving a job.[218] Often mocked as "gag rules," nondisclosures have faced widespread criticism for shielding companies from public accusations of wrongdoing, including sexual misconduct, racism, or discriminatory treatment. Leyva's

---

218   Kari Paul, "California bill targets NDAs that prevent workers from speaking about discrimination," *The Guardian,* February 10, 2021, https://www.theguardian.com/us-news/2021/feb/10/california-sb331-nda-harassment-discrimination.

bill, known as the Silenced No More Act, would expand current California protections against secret workplace settlements, further prohibiting their use for employees when leaving a company. The proposed law builds on a previous law banning their use to keep quiet allegations of sexual harassment.

Explains the senator, "It is unacceptable for any employer to try to silence a worker because he or she was a victim of any type of harassment or discrimination—whether due to race, sexual orientation, religion, age or any other characteristic....[and passage of this law] will empower survivors to speak out—if they so wish—so they can hold perpetrators accountable and hopefully prevent abusers from continuing to torment and abuse other workers."

In addition to legal and financial restrictions, nondisclosure agreements can also have substantial emotional effects. People experiencing harassment are further isolated, unable to share their experiences even with those close to them, or to communicate with their fellow workers what they have experienced on the job. The emotional toll can be severe: imagine leaving your job and not being able to tell anyone—even your spouse—details of how you were discriminated against. Would we expect a rape survivor to have to "keep quiet"? Yet this is, essentially, what happens with nondisclosure agreements. The gag order and secrecy surrounding settlement agreements can result in psychological trauma on top of the initial abuse and discrimination one has endured. Yet, faced with undergoing years of litigation and exorbitant attorney fees that most working women simply don't have, it is no wonder that many women choose to agree to a settlement despite odious consequences.

Indeed, activism starts with awareness and a backbone to be the change we want to see, because what we now see is so blatantly obvious that it's amazing it's even taken us this long. As Sheryl Sandberg and Adam Grant point out, "there is no evidence girls or women are any meaner than men; rather, there's the expectation of how they *should* act. Women are just expected to be nicer. We stereotype men as aggressive and women as kind. When women violate those stereotypes, we judge them harshly. 'A man has to be Joe McCarthy to be called ruthless,' Marlo Thomas once lamented. 'All a woman has to do is put you on hold.'"[219]

You know that saying, "If a fly on the wall could talk…" about what goes on in conference rooms everywhere? Well, I don't care about the fly, but every time I see an image of our symbol of justice—a *woman*—she's typically depicted as blindfolded, right? Well, I wonder what she has seen, and what she would have to say and if she's ever felt like just dropping those scales of justice that have rarely weighed equal for too many sisters I've known, and just scream in her best

---

219 Sheryl Sandberg and Adam Grant, "Sheryl Sandberg on the Myth of the Catty Woman," *New York Times*, June 23, 2016, https://www.nytimes.com/2016/06/23/opinion/sunday/sheryl-sandberg-on-the-myth-of-the-catty-woman.html.

and loudest "bitch" voice: "Enough! *Ya Basta!* The jig is up!" But she's an icon: our symbol that justice will prevail; we are only human. We can do that, and when we do, we will become the voice that we long to hear.

And once those alleged "mean, bossy, bitchy, catty, aggressive" women start documenting, and talking, and blogging, and filing our claims, and challenging a system that is programmed to discriminate against women for another century or more, those glass ceilings and labyrinths will become shattered and dismantled. It is our time to act.

Once upon a time, I was summoned to a conference room and told that I was a "mismatch" by corporate suits. You know what is a mismatch? The continued discrimination, sexism, gender bias, and stereotyping of women who, simply because we are who we are and unafraid to be strong, are then deemed *just not that likable* on presumed personality characteristics *a quarter century* after Ann Hopkins's tenacious battle to smash the highest legal glass ceiling in America. Let's teach our daughters (and sons), sisters (and brothers) the true meaning of the word. Those ceilings, and labyrinths, and Hollywood imagery still persist, but this book is a call to arms to bring them down because, ultimately, all women pay the price for gender bias.

It is time for us to Act Up—for Ann Hopkins; Act Up for all women who have previously stepped forward to tell their stories and file their claims, win or lose; Act Up for ourselves, for our daughters and sisters, and under a Constitution and a growing body of social science research and law that recognizes and respects us for the tenacity and strength of our character.

Bossy? Bitchy? Bombastic? You say tomato, I say tomato: Strong. Tenacious. Fearless.

Photo of Gloria Romero with her daughter, Soledad, at a 1993 remembrance march for UFW co-founder and leader Cesar Chavez. Standing with them is feminist icon "Betita" Martinez